THE LAW IN
BLACK
AND
WHITE
AND THE
YELLOW
IN BETWEEN

THE LAW IN
BLACK
AND
WHITE
AND THE
YELLOW
IN BETWEEN

An Asian lawyer's experience of the law in a Western world

BY

Raymond W. H. Tan

"We are what we think, all that we are arises from our thoughts, with our thoughts we make the world."

– Buddha

Publishing Services by Happy Self Publishing
www.happyselfpublishing.com

Year: 2019

This book focuses on Australian law, and in particular, Western Australia law where the practice of Tan and Tan Lawyers is located.

This book is dedicated to my wife and soulmate Annie Sim. I thank her for sharing my dreams and for helping me fulfil them. I also dedicate this book to my two sons, Jazton and Tyzton, and I hope I can call them to the Western Australian Bar when the time comes.

Happy Self Publishing.

Acknowledgments

I thank my wife, Annie and my sons for supporting me in this endeavour. Many clients of Tan and Tan Lawyers are to be thanked for their support when I discussed writing this book, including the title of the book.

Thanks to my niece Liz and my sis Rinda for encouraging me to finish this book. Being writers themselves, their help pushed me to the finish line.

Most important, my departed brother Charles for showing me that the love of the law is a noble quest.

I also want to thank my first legal masters namely, Teo Soh Lung, Lai Maylene and Lee Kim Huay for showing me that the law is not about making money but about the need to help the less fortunate.

Table of Contents

Chapter 4: A Great Estate - What You Owe Your Family 77

Foreword

As a young man in the early 1980's, Raymond came to our little law firm of three women lawyers through the introduction of his eldest brother, Charles. Soon he became involved in everything the firm did - from typing documents on manual typewriters to filing court papers, serving documents and carrying out research. There was nothing that he found too humble or difficult to do. He was the ideal articled clerk!

Raymond's dream of becoming a lawyer through articled clerkship ended abruptly when the Singapore legal profession, without any prior notice, ceased the practice of accepting articled clerks into the profession. Undeterred and with the help of his siblings, he flew off to London to obtain his law degree. I am therefore very happy that he is now a successful lawyer in Perth.

The Law In Black And White And The Yellow In Between is a general guide to the law in Western Australia and a delightful account of the author's life. It is a helpful book that gives practical tips on how to set up a business and get a pay rise, how to ensure security for your family and settle family disputes. It also touches on immigration and criminal law. The book discusses practical problems and issues that most of us would encounter at some time in our lives. But it is in no way a substitute for the services of lawyers as the author cautions throughout his book.

Reading about his tough life as a child and how he and his streetwise elder brother sold bananas outside the market despite it being illegal to hawk without a licence, I can understand the core values of Raymond. He knows what life is all about – risk-taking, achievements and the importance of sharing knowledge as he does with this book.

Raymond is philosophical. He is concerned not only with the well-being of his family and friends but also with society. He raises funds for the homeless by participating in the St Vinnies CEO Sleepout.

It is remarkable that at the age of 50, Raymond has made it a point to pause in life and write this book. He is generous in sharing his knowledge and I am sure that anyone who wants to have a general idea of the law will find this book helpful.

Teo Soh Lung
Singapore

Endorsements

Believe it or not, there's more to being a lawyer than just knowing the law. Raymond Tan uses his own personal and cultural perspective and life-long experience to go behind the scenes and explain how and why lawyers do what they do. With real-life examples, he takes you on a journey of his own and his clients' experiences in everyday situations. Answers to your questions on what to do, what not, why and anything in-between!

HEINRICH MOSER
Barrister - Arbitrator -Mediator Western Australia.

"The Law in Black and White and the Yellow in Between" is a 'magnum opus' and a testament of Raymond's experience beyond law! I love it right from the start; it's entertaining, very interesting and engaging. For someone remotely interested in law, this book summarises comprehensively the Western

Australian laws covering many facets of life and offers *much more...* The 'pearls of wisdom' in this book is a treasure trove which will benefit the international audience. I love Raymond's ability to humanise the law, which is highly inspirational. It's a 'must-read' even for the wider audience, 'knowledge is power', not just specifically targeted at those interested in law.

THK TENG
Senior Research Fellow,
National Heart Centre Singapore
Adjunct Research Fellow, School of Population
& Global Health, University of Western Australia

This is a book no-one should pass up who is remotely interested in learning how the law works and how it can work for the reader's benefit.

I have been the beneficiary of Raymond's generous spirit when I wanted to set up a Foundation for Healing from Abuse. This didn't eventuate, but if I had been thinking along the lines of Raymond's mind, it might have had a better chance.

Raymond writes with a lawyer's precise mind. His is not a story but an accurate presentation in a very readable style, of what we should all know by the time we are old enough to have a job or enter into any kind of contract, formal or informal.

CARLA van RAAY,
author of *God's Callgirl* Perth

When I am having a quiet, reflective moment and my mind drifts off to the legal profession, always, without exception, I remember the quotation from Shakespeare's Henry VI, "The first thing we do, let's kill all the lawyers". The only quotation of poetry I remember. But there are exceptions to all rules, and Raymond Tan is one of those exceptions. His life journey, as recorded in his book, Singapore to London to Perth, and points in between, shows that rare individual that strives against the odds to follow a path that was built upon challenge after challenge to become a lawyer. Not just any lawyer, but Raymond Tan, the lawyer. One who has a deep commitment to the wider society, and to use his knowledge of the law, and his basic humanity, to help others, and never forgetting where he came from. Read "The Law in Black and White and the Yellow in Between" not for an insight into the law, but for inspiration.

HAJI ROMZI FAIZAL (RON GRANT)
CEO, Cocos Islands Cooperative Society Ltd
Cocos (Keeling) islands

This book succinctly summarises those Western Australian laws which are the most relevant in our everyday life. You could even treat it as *"the Beginner's Guide on WA's Laws"*! As a former legal practitioner and someone who worked with Raymond in his firm for about 10 years, reading this book has brought some fond memories back for me about the legal profession and more importantly, about Raymond's family. Annie, Jazton, Tyzton and, Raymond are a brilliant team and they have been ably supported by his extended family, including his mother, mother-in-law and his brother Charles. Not only did Raymond teach me about the practice of law, he's taught me how to be a lawyer with integrity, how to be a decent person, and how to be a good husband and father (and he also spent 6 years teaching me how to write proper English!).

THE HONOURABLE PIERRE YANG

Nobel Peace Prize winner and former UN Secretary-General Kofi Annan said, *"Knowledge is power, information is liberating. Education is the premise of progress, in every society, in every family."* The Law in Black and White and Yellow in Between provides a very practical and informative guide to the law, as well as a charming insight into Raymond Tan's life. Raymond's altruistic nature shines through the pages with excellent advice written in a clear, precise and entertaining manner. A must read for anyone wishing to have a sound control of their affairs covering the many facets of the law which we all will encounter in our everyday lives.

JENNIFER MERIGAN
Editor
Have a Go News
Perth WA

To the many people migrating to Australia to establish themselves and their families in what they hope will be better lives, the Australian legal system replaces the legal system with which they have been familiar in a different language and cultural environment.

Necessary contact with the Australian legal system brings with it that natural human reaction, fear of the unknown.

Raymond Tan's book brings a humanity to the legal process, which is reassuring, and, with the addition of much useful information, educates and addresses that fear of the unknown.

Mr Tan's intention is well expressed in the title of his book and has been well achieved.

SEAN O'SULLIVAN
Barrister
Perth

Raymond's book shows how to be a good lawyer. His legal practice motto is looking after his clients' interests and saving them money. These tenets have enabled his firm to grow from strength to strength as a stirring example of law, in society. It reflects the principles of compassion, respect and of fairness that has marked his whole life. Just as Raymond is proud of his sons, so too am I, one of his first "bosses", exceedingly proud of him as a humane, intelligent, generous and skilled professional of the global legal community. This book with its practical advice on the law is a testament of his continued contribution and service to his community. Perth is indeed fortunate to have him in their midst.

LAI MAYLENE, formerly:
Partner, Teo, Lai & Lee Singapore; Barrister & Solicitor, Nigel Dunlop Christchurch; Barrister & Solicitor, Buddle Findlay Auckland; Risk Manager, Bell Gully Auckland

Introduction

Everyone needs to know about the law so they can protect themselves. However, often, by the time you see a lawyer for advice, it may be too late. This book hopes to enlighten the reader with the general concepts of the law and how to use them to their advantage.

It is not intended to provide complete legal advice for your particular circumstance or replace the need for a lawyer.

I am the Yellow between the Black and White of the written law. An Asian lawyer practising in a Western world. I may have a different perspective from a Western lawyer. If that perspective helps you in getting a better understanding of the law, then the book has achieved its aim.

This is not intended to be a serious book about the law and how it affects you. The book should give you a commonsense approach to the law. It also gives you insight into my personal life as a lawyer along with some anecdotes related to the law.

CHAPTER I

The Making of a Lawyer.

FROM THE STREETS OF TIONG BAHRU, SINGAPORE TO PERTH, WESTERN AUSTRALIA

My name is Raymond W. H. Tan and I will be your tour guide for this ride around the amusement park known as life and law. I know what you're thinking: "Who is this Raymond guy, and why should I listen to him?" I am a Chinese lawyer trying to blend traditional Eastern values with our constantly evolving Western Australian legal terrain.

I am well versed in the law and the art of negotiation. Perhaps, more important, I understand the spirit of the law: That place between black and white, where nuance, street smarts, and wise counsel matter most. I hope my experiences in life and law will help you navigate the sometimes choppy waters of your own life.

I am the owner of Tan and Tan Lawyers Pty Ltd., and I am grateful to all my staff (especially Kenneth) for their hard work and their assistance in the writing of this book.

When I wrote the first chapter, I had just celebrated my fiftieth birthday. Turning fifty causes a man to examine who he is, where he has been, and where he wants to go. So who am I?

Like many of you, I am a husband, father, brother and son.

I am Chinese.

I am an Australian permanent resident with citizenship beckoning.

I know the immigrant's song.

I have sold bananas at a Singapore market at eight years old, been a construction labourer at twelve years of age, a flower delivery man, taught at a primary school, and worked full-time as an office boy while attending night school for my high school education. The list goes on.

I grew up in Singapore, the ninth child in a family of ten. My father drove a taxi, and my mother was a seamstress. Mum and Dad were understandably busy making ends meet, so my siblings and I had the freedom to hang around the neighbourhood.

We lived in Tiong Bahru (which in any country would be considered a slum in the sixties) in state housing low-rise apartments. Tiong Bahru is now an upmarket inner suburb. The building I grew up in used to be called the 'Four Story Tiong Bahru Flats'. It has since been renovated and converted into a hotel called the Link Hotel. You might have had the pleasure of staying there during a trip to Singapore.

Dad taught me to enjoy life whatever the situation. I will always treasure the many sacrifices he made bringing up our family. I do remember him buying papayas for the family, and that was the only dessert we would usually have. There was never any ice cream or cakes. When I tell my children this, they say that we could not have been that poor as we could afford papayas, which are expensive in Australia. Papayas are cheap as anything in Singapore. Sadly, Dad passed away on 9 Mar 1988 leaving Mum to be cared for mainly by brothers Lawrence, Wee Seng and my sisters Belinda and Serene and all their spouses who live in Singapore. I owe them all a life gratitude for their care of Mum as the other siblings lived in Western Australia.

When my family was living there, contractors used to bring their sewing work to the apartment compound to hand over to people who wanted to do the work. They were selective and usually rude and overbearing since one's livelihood could depend on their generosity.

I remember Mum pleading to do the work for them. She would splash water on her eyes to stay awake and complete the sewing. My mum's work supported the family substantially. She also used to frequent pawnshops to pawn her jewelry when funds were short. Mum would give the pawnshop her jewelry, and in return, they would give her a handwritten ticket in Chinese. In the 1970s, a pawn ticket of about $30 Singapore could feed the family of ten for an entire month.

Mum's example of love, hard work, and sacrifice stays with me every day. I have a collage of her pawn tickets. They are framed and sitting with pride of place in my office conference room to honour her sacrifice to the family as she never had the money to redeem the pawned items. I still remember showing her the collage in my office conference room. Her first comment was "why do you want to display our impoverished past to all your clients". My answer is that I am proud of where I have come from. Sadly, Mum passed away in her sleep on 15 September 2019 before I could have the book printed and presented to her. Her passing has left a big hole in the Tan family. Brothers Lawrence, Wee Seng, and sisters Belinda and Serene have done so much to ensure her last few years were as comfortable as possible. Their spouses especially Irene, Chok Mui, Henry and Kenneth and, their children have also always supported them in the care of my Mum. Mum is survived by 9 children, 24 grandchildren and, 10 great-grandchildren.

While Mum worked, we kids were left to our own devices in a rough and tumble neighbourhood. Tiong Bahru is a suburb in Singapore, notorious for being the playground of gangsters.

Life in Tiong Bahru taught me to be streetwise. Some of my earliest memories are of hanging around a banana warehouse when I was only ten with my brother Lawrence, who was a year older than me. The warehouse had bananas delivered in bulk from Malaysia. We helped the labourers unload the bunches of bananas. and as payment, we would get the leftover bananas to bring home.

Lawrence and I used to set up a stall in the Tiong Bahru markets to sell the bananas for spare cash. Selling bananas without a proper stall is called 'hawking', which is an offence. The authorities had Environmental Officers who were there to make sure there were no hawkers in the market. Every time an officer was spotted, all the hawkers would make a run for it. This game of cat and mouse was great fun when we were kids, but not something I would recommend as it is illegal. We were minors and reckless. I knew nothing of the law then.

Those early experiences as a child banana 'outlaw' helped point me towards my career. By the age of 15, I knew I wanted to be a lawyer. Lawrence, despite his lack of a university degree, has prospered as a developer/project manager, largely through his street-smarts. Whenever I interview new employees, I am always more interested if they are street-smart. Any graduate who supported themselves will, I am sure, have more knowledge and experience compared to a full-time student cocooned from the world of business and life.

*****

While my adventures with Lawrence were teaching me street-smarts, my older brother, Charles, was busy becoming a lawyer. He became my inspiration and first mentor in the law.

Charles was called to the bar in Singapore and was well known as a criminal trial lawyer. Without hesitation, looking up to my big brother was why I became interested in the law. Sadly, Charles passed away on the 11th of June 2016. He is sadly missed by his wife, Cynthia, and his children Timothy, Vicky, and Elizabeth.

Elizabeth is a published writer and has inspired me to finish this book. I was also surprised to discover my sister, Rinda, is also writing a book. What can I say? We may be a family of writers!

I also owe my law degree to the sacrifices made by my family members who helped support me during the times I was studying in the United Kingdom.

A special mention should be made of my brother, Wee Seng, who taught me the value of money and how to invest. My other brother Stewart taught me that spiritual values are as important, if not more so than material wealth.

All my sisters taught me that family is the most important.

My dearest mum, in front of her collage of pawn tickets that takes pride of place in my conference room.

Right Livelihood: Buddhism and the Law

I am a practising Buddhist. My faith touches all areas of my life. The fifth principle on the Buddhist Eightfold Path is Right Livelihood. Right Livelihood cautions us not to do business that is dishonest or harmful to others. This means a person's calling should be motivated by a love for humanity, not a desire for power or money. I did not become a lawyer to make money or to hurt others. I wanted to help the less fortunate who cannot defend themselves.

Applying Buddhist virtues to my law practice and businesses requires some meditation. I once attended a lecture by Ajahn Brahm, the Abbott of the Bodhinyana Monastery based in Perth. He was discussing Buddhism and how it applies to corporate Australia. His words and advice were most reassuring. He recited a short story from Leo Tolstoy so applicable to all aspects of life, including the practice of the law. The story was about an emperor who sought the philosophy of life. He ended up with three simple questions:

1. When is the most important time?
2. Who is the most important person?
3. What is the most important thing to do?

The answer to the first question is NOW. NOW is the only time we have. If you wish to thank your receptionist for the good work she has done, NOW is the time. If you dwell in the past or worry about the future, you will miss most of your life.

The answer to the second question is the person standing in front of you requesting your attention. We rarely give our full attention to the person speaking to us. If all couples practised the answer to this second question, the world's divorce rate would drop.

The answer to the final question is TO CARE. Unless we care about what we are doing and why we are doing it, then there is no reason for us to function. Likewise, unless we care about what we are doing for our clients, we will never be good lawyers.

CHAPTER 2

The Legal Profession

Legal work is exciting. Each day my practice brings me a new challenge. I am always guided by my desire to help people. I am amazed at the myriad of problems my clients face. My role is to solve problems for my clients. That is a big reason I love the law.

How to Talk to Your Lawyer

Now you know why I became a lawyer. And you know that lawyers are problem-solvers. This may surprise you. I have occasionally heard people say they want to hire a 'bulldog' to represent them. Influenced by television lawyers with explosive fantasy courtroom scenes, they imagine that a brash, loud-talking lawyer will do the job.

Nothing is further from the truth. A good lawyer has to be cool-headed, not a hothead. They have to have their wits about them when all around them are "losing theirs and blaming it on you," to paraphrase Rudyard Kipling. A good lawyer is book smart and streetwise.

Being streetwise due to my upbringing has helped me substantially in my work as a lawyer. I recall a case where a client claimed he paid $300,000 in cash to a friend and was suing his friend for the return of the money. I asked if he had any witnesses to this transaction. A few days later, the client brought in another friend who was supposed to have seen my client handing over the $300,000 to the friend he wanted to sue.

I questioned this witness at length about what he had seen. I asked him, "Do you know how long it takes to count $300,000 in $100 bills?" I know it takes a long time as I have seen it being counted before in another case.

This witness could not confirm how long the counting process took. After substantial questioning, the witness admitted that he never saw the transaction. He was lying. If I were not streetwise, I probably would not have caught out the witness, and he may have lied in the courtroom.

Being a lawyer requires us to read a lot and be able to communicate our thoughts and reasoning to judges and fellow lawyers. However, we also need to communicate our advice to our client. If we cannot break the advice down into simple and understandable English, we will be failing in our service to our client.

Interviewing techniques are also crucial when we see clients. Being streetwise helps a lawyer understand what to ask and how to make sure the client is telling the truth. It helps us discover things about the case that the client does not even know are important.

These tactics may make you nervous about dealing with lawyers. I know from experience that many people are intimidated by their lawyer, even if they have known them for a long time. Communication between a lawyer and client is essential. Here are seven tips on how to handle a visit with a lawyer.

1. *Be in Control of Your Emotions.* Your lawyer's job is to give you advice not influenced by emotion. Your own emotions can cloud your view of the problem and how to fix it. Your lawyer will try to have you step back from your problem during the visit to get a different perspective on the issue. Sometimes, clients wonder why their lawyer shows little

emotion while discussing the case. Think of it this way: imagine you are in a swamp full of crocodiles. If I'm in the swamp with you, then I can't help you. I need to be on the riverbank so I can tell you to turn left or right when the crocodiles are coming.

2. *Trust Your Lawyer.* It is the lawyer's duty to maintain the confidence of his or her client. In return, they will ask that you listen to what they have to say and listen to their advice. Remember, you are paying the lawyer for their expertise. If you spend your time and money on a particular lawyer, you should be able to trust them. If you can't, find another lawyer and avoid wasting both your time and, more important, money.

3. *Be Honest and Do Not Leave Out Any Details.* Like trust, honesty is an important part of any lawyer/client relationship. If your lawyer asks you for any information related to your case, give it to them so they can do their job to the best of their ability. Be prepared, to tell the truth! Lawyers have experience in dealing with people, and many are skilled at spotting a lie. It is better to be honest with your lawyer than to go to court and be caught out there! Even if the information is embarrassing to you or you are afraid it will hurt your case,

your lawyer can deal with the issue better if he knows about it upfront and can control it, rather than having the truth surface at an inopportune time.

4. *Ask for Clarification.* Many clients are unfamiliar with legal terminology. Your lawyer should be able to break things down so you can understand them. There is no point in listening if you don't understand, so just ask them to simplify. If they can't do this, get another lawyer.

5. *Don't Feel Intimidated.* Again, a lawyer with good communication skills and the ability to relate to people should not leave you feeling intimidated. Remember, they are there to act in your best interests, and obtaining a favourable outcome for you is their number one priority. Even when they ask you difficult questions, remember, the lawyer is on your side!

6. *Be Organised and Be Prepared.* A hot tip is to make a mind map of all your questions before you see your lawyer. If you take three hours to do this at home, think about how much longer (and more expensive) your visit to your lawyer will be if you wait until you get there to do it! If you have your list of questions ready, a lawyer can read it in ten

minutes rather than spending a few expensive hours at the office. They will then probably know straight away what needs to be done. Also, you will not risk forgetting the points you need to make if you think about it beforehand.

7. *Calling Your Lawyer.* If you have a concern, a question, or need something clarified, it is a good reason to call your lawyer. However, it is not a good idea to call them five times about the same issue. Remember, the lawyer has to charge you each time you call them. A great option is to take advantage of email if your lawyer permits it. It saves your lawyer time and saves you money.

Frequently Asked Questions About Lawyers

Since the practice of law often seems mysterious and complicated to non-lawyers, I've answered some frequently asked questions about the practice of law.

How does one find a good lawyer? Unfortunately, there is no national rating system or guide to help you figure out who is the best lawyer for you. The first thing you should look for is a lawyer who specialises in the law you need help with. If you do not know which type of law addresses your problem, then you should call a lawyer referral service for advice. The local legal aid offices are a good start. They can point you in the right direction. A good way to find a lawyer is to ask your friends and family members who they would recommend, just as you would with a mechanic or a plumber.

How does one assess the quality of a lawyer? It is hard to assess the standard and quality of a lawyer without a rating system to show the public the level of the lawyer's expertise. However, the Law Society of Western Australia developed the Quality Practice Standard ("QPS") to recognise WA Law firms that strive to provide superior service standards to their clients. These firms have implemented regulated internal procedures and practices to better protect and serve the interest of their clients.

In August 2010, Tan and Tan Lawyers became the 44th law firm in Perth to be accredited. We were one of only two firms that received accreditation on their first attempt. The accredited firms have all gone through a lengthy process of streamlining and implementing internal procedures to ensure their services remain at consistently high standards. The Quality Practice Standard exceeds the legal requirements of the State laws regarding operating law practices. The law firms accredited are audited each year to ensure that they remain compliant with the standards. Tan and Tan Lawyers authorised use of the QPS Logo means that clients are assured that Tan and Tan Lawyers maintain a high standard of service.

The Law Society of Western Australia certifies that QPS accredited firms can better serve their clients by:

- Adopting modern quality management principles;
- Focusing on clients' requirements and client care; and
- Striving for consistency of service for all clients by all at the firm.

This ensures that a QPS law firm is efficient, which saves you money. Look for the QPS logo when assessing which lawyer to hire because it is one of the few ways that consumers are told which law firms are above board.

Why do lawyers always say, "It Depends?" Clients wonder why lawyers never seem to give a simple answer to a question straight away. "It depends" seems evasive until you consider it this way: imagine you are buying new golf clubs. You walk into the store and ask the expert what to buy. Does he immediately tell you which set of clubs to purchase? No. First, he will ask you how long you have been playing? What kind of clubs do you play with now? How long are you off the tee? What is your best shot? What do you most want to improve? Once the golf pro knows more about you and your golf game, he can then narrow your options to the best set of clubs for your game. Then he can give you his recommendation, leaving the final decision to you. A good lawyer will do the same thing as the golf expert—diagnose the problem and figure out the best options for solving it. Just don't ask your lawyer for putting tips!

What is the difference between a barrister and a solicitor?
I am sometimes asked what the difference is between a Barrister and a Solicitor. Traditionally, countries that derived their legal system from English common law split the legal profession into two groups. In England, a Barrister predominantly goes to court to argue cases. Barristers are the ones you see wearing robes and powdered wigs. Conversely, a solicitor works directly with clients, giving advice and drafting legal documents (solicitors get to wear their own hair!). The Solicitor is not given the right of audience in the Courts other than the lower courts. Barristers, therefore, are instructed by Solicitors to represent the Solicitor's clients when matters go to trial. The paperwork preparing for a trial is usually

done by the Solicitor. Barristers do not see clients other than through a referral from a Solicitor.

In New South Wales and Queensland, there is still a split profession. But in South Australia, Victoria, Western Australia, and the Australian Capital Territory, the legal profession is fused in that a lawyer like me can work as a Barrister or a Solicitor. Some lawyers decide they only want to do Barrister's work. Hence, they practice in an office called the Bar Chambers (we are informed that the Bar Chambers do not dispense alcohol, though we have our suspicions).

Here's a snippet of legal history for you. The next time you see a lawyer in court wearing one of their black gowns, you will notice a pouch-like pocket at the back of their gowns. One theory is that the pouch was used by clients to place the Barrister's honorarium (or fees) as it was beneath the Barrister to be handed money directly. The world has changed since those times. Nowadays, the pouches are sealed as we expect cheques or cash. We have also stopped wearing wigs since 2010. These wigs made from horsehair were never comfortable.

CHAPTER 3

Business Transactions

Feng Shui is the ancient Chinese aesthetic art designed to orient man-made structures to stimulate positive 'Qi'. Qi (pronounced Chi) means energy or life force. Feng Shui draws on traditional astronomy and cosmology to help people make important decisions and organise their life so it is auspicious. I consult my Feng Shui master when making important business decisions, including when to move, how to arrange the office, and whether the buildings I work in will bring positive Qi. When Tan and Tan Lawyers made the big move from Wellington Street to Terrace Road in East Perth, my Feng Shui master, Kieran O'Hara, advised of the best date to start. He also designed the whole office layout for optimum Feng Shui benefit.

I always try to combine best practices, old and new, in all areas of my life. I also have a 'business doctor,' Jeff Miles, who offers suggestions to take my law firm to the next level. He encouraged me to get a bigger office and to expand my practice to a satellite office. My close friend Ming, graphic designer and marketing guru from www.wekyso.com.au (We Knock your Socks Off), has also helped me move upwards in my vision of what an ideal law business should be.

Today's work environment is always changing. What follows are some of my favourite tips for improving your life, whether as an entrepreneur, manager or worker. Never be afraid to take chances and ask experts old and new what they know.

Being Your Own Boss

Tan and Tan Lawyers have been advising clients on their business purchases for many years. My greatest joy is seeing a client about to go from being employed to self-employed. I love coaching them on the right way to buy a business and what to look out for. This chapter discusses all the ways to be your own boss. For those of you who will remain employed for whatever reason, don't worry—I have tips on how to avoid major potholes and make your work life more bearable.

I've practised law for over 29 years. That is a long time in dog years. When I was called to the Bar, my primary thoughts were about working as a practising lawyer. Eventually, I ended up as the CEO of my own law firm, which means, I manage people and run a business besides handling cases. In the last ten years, Tan and Tan Lawyers has more than doubled its staff and expanded its real estate and settlement business. Running my own law firm is an enormous challenge, but the rewards are great. My family remains the most important in my life. However, I am so grateful to the great employees that enjoy working at Tan and Tan Lawyers, and my clients who appreciate the work we do. I enjoy my work every day and the ability to play golf every weekend.

Golf? What has golf do with the law, you may ask? One pleasure of having one's own business is that you can control your own time. For many years, I have been able to take a Thursday afternoon off most weeks to play golf with my buddies Henry, Frank, and Rick. If you were employed, what is the chance of doing that on your boss's time?

The other side of the coin is that being your own boss means you will probably be busier than ever before. But you can do it as long as:

a) you have business systems in place;
b) can delegate your work;
c) you manage your time appropriately.

How do you know if being your own boss is the right move for you? One important consideration is whether you are happy when you go to work each day. I am fortunate because I love my job. If you are one of the many people who dread going to work, have you ever thought of starting your own business?

Being self-employed requires a broad range of skills, but it can provide many benefits. One may earn a better living, as being in business can provide you with some beneficial tax laws. Being your own boss also gives you a greater feeling of control over your work destiny and outcomes. However, you are also ultimately responsible for your failures.

Another strong reason to work for yourself is the opportunity to develop your own creative ideas. Fulfilling your own plan gives you full rein for how you want to develop your own business, and this is especially true if you have identified a niche in the market you believe you can fill. Last, but not least, being your own boss is an excellent way to build a business asset you can leave to your family or assist with your retirement if it is sold.

Sounds good, doesn't it? Before you hand in your resignation, let's talk about some disadvantages. Although there are various advantages to starting your own business, it is not for everybody.

To help picture business ownership realistically, an unfortunate fact is that 60% of companies fail within the first five years, so by no means is it always plain sailing. But if you go into business with your eyes open and have calculated your risk, then it is an educated choice.

There are also issues you should consider, starting with long working hours, which can lead to physical and mental stress and strain. This is especially true in the first years of the business. You will have a high level of responsibility because you only answer to yourself.

You are also the sole decision-maker, which is why it is vital that you have legal and accounting advice you can trust.

You must get the right accounting and legal advice before you go into business. A good accountant should be able to go through different corporate structures and tax benefits. As with lawyers, there are accountants, and there are accountants.

You need an accountant, not just a bean counter. You need an accountant with good business and investment experience. I always believe that before you engage an accountant or lawyer, you need to ask them for their own life and investment experience. If you wish to be a property baron, you do not want to see a lawyer or accountant who has not accumulated a property portfolio. I have worked well with Lillian Fisher from Chan and Naylor Accountants, Perth, for a few years. We are both property investors, and hence, have tried to keep on top of the investment game. I strongly believe that being in business is just a stepping stone for going into property investment. As the Former Mcdonald's CFO Harry J Sonneborn is quoted as saying, "we are not technically in the food business. We are in the real estate business". .

Being in business means there is no steady pay cheque, and your income will vary. You may even need to live from other resources (from family, partner or spouse) until the business is profitable. There may be hidden costs associated with your business, such as public liability insurance.

Don't forget that when you leave behind the stress from your former boss, you also wave goodbye to employee benefits, such as holiday pay and sick leave. Unless the new boss — you — have set up a good system, you will be watching your employees take leave while you are stuck with your nose to the grindstone.

Still wondering whether to hand in your resignation letter so you can start your own business? Consider these questions before taking that step towards independence.

- *What business will I be involved in*? What are my skills? What have I got that is special? Speak to your friends and professionals.
- *What information do I have about the industry?* You will be surprised what kind of information you can find on the internet. Do your research!
- *Have I prepared a business plan that deals with issues of employment, marketing, sales, and financial management?* If you are in Western Australia, check out http://www.sbdc.com.au where you will find a wealth of information for free. Do you need staff? What are the rules for hiring and firing? Check out the rules at http://www.fairwork.gov.au

- *What training is available to help me gain skills and knowledge in areas I am not familiar with?* You may be the best baker in Perth, but if you want to set up a bakery, you will also need to know about accounting and management.

- *Do I have enough funding?* Do you have sufficient funds for your personal needs until the business generates a surplus? How much money can you put into the business? It is often a good idea to prepare a statement of assets and liabilities to discover what money can be borrowed and, if need be, locate a finance broker who can assist you in getting funding to kick-start the business. Check the location and whether you are leasing the premises. Can you work from home first?

- *Am I prepared?* The most important thing when starting a business is to make sure you have thought everything through. A lack of adequate planning is the main cause of most small business failures, so prepare a business plan or you will not understand what you are doing. Check out which intellectual properties need to be protected and what legal issues you will need to cover—this can be a minefield! Investigate issues regarding trademarks, business names, superannuation rules and taxes, and research what licenses and permits are needed. You do not want to run afoul of the law.

*****

Business Structures and Business Names

Some of you have probably read the tips above and concluded that running your own business is not for you. There's nothing wrong with that. I have some advice for you on how to get more out of your current job—just skip ahead and discover how to get yourself a raise!

As for the hardy few that have taken the plunge towards self-employment, congratulations! You have taken the first step in daring to challenge yourself and your destiny. You have told yourself to chase your dreams. You have dared to believe in yourself and your ability to achieve more than you ever could as an employee. However, let's sort some infrastructure out before we make that journey into self-employment. Being daring and being prudent and calculating your risk are different matters.

Let's sort out some infrastructure you should use before you trade. It is important to lay the right corporate foundation for your business before you actually trade. There are many things to consider before you start that climb toward success. Sole proprietorship/partnership and business names are but two. Most businesses are organised as either a sole proprietorship or a partnership arrangement.

What business name do you register?

Always carefully check that the business name you want to use is original. The Australian Business Registry has a computerised list of all names registered in Australia, and it is available for inspection at the Business Names Branch. You should not incur expenses (print business cards, letterheads, etc.) regarding a business name until you have confirmed its availability and registered the name.

When Should You Register a Business Name?

Carrying on a business or forming a partnership does not necessarily mean that the name or names should be registered as a business name. For example, if you are John Smith and you wish to trade as John Smith, there is no need to register a business name. However, if the business is not your usual name, or if it involves any additional words, then a business name needs to be registered.

You need to go to the Australian Securities and Investments Commission website at www.asic.gov.au to check if the name is available.

How Long is the Registered Business Name Valid For?

The registration of a business name remains in force for three years. It may be renewed one month before or one month after the expiration of the registration. Keep tabs on the renewal datelines. Failure to re-register may enable someone else registering the name for their own use.

What Other Alternatives are there to Using a Business Name?

Speak to a lawyer and an accountant to discover if using a business name is the right business structure for your purposes. Lawyers will look at it from a legal perspective. The biggest concern about trading under a business name is that you become personally liable for the debts of the business. That means that if the business fails, the creditors can pursue you by getting court orders to sell your personal assets. It is sometimes safer to use a company structure. Your accountant's advice should be sought before you register either a business name or proprietary limited company ('Pty Ltd').

Benefits of Using a Proprietary Limited Structure

It is now possible to incorporate a Pty Ltd company with one shareholder and one director. It is basically a legal fiction allowed by the law. We say it is a legal fiction in that the director meets with himself when decisions are made by the Board of the Pty Ltd Company.

One of the main benefits is there is a limited personal liability if you use the Pty Ltd structure. That means if the Pty Ltd Company fails, the creditors cannot usually sue the directors or shareholders.

There are certain circumstances where the directors and shareholders can be sued personally for the debts of the Pty Ltd Company. For example

- Where the directors give personal guarantees to the creditors.
- Where the creditors can show that the directors were trading while the company was insolvent and unable to pay its debts.

Tax Liabilities

Speak to your accountant or lawyer if you are considering changing over from a sole proprietorship or partnership using a business name to a Pty Ltd Company. The duties of shareholders and/or directors are numerous and should be considered carefully before a Pty Ltd Company is set up.

Australian Business Number

Under current tax legislation, all businesses should have an Australian Business Number (ABN). You may use the company's ABN with your company's name in place of the company's Australian Company Number (ACN) on company documents and negotiable instruments, provided that

    a.   Your ABN includes your nine-digit ACN.

    b.   The quotation of the ABN is as necessary as the quotation of the ACN in all your business documents. For example, a company must place its ACN with its name on the first page where that name occurs in a document.

*****

Doing Business in the 21st Century: Intellectual Property and Domain Names

By now, everyone knows that the internet is a crucial part of doing business in the new millennium. However, many people don't consider what other corporate information is proprietary. It is best to understand intellectual property and have a sit down with a lawyer to discuss the implications for your own business. Here are the most frequently asked questions about intellectual property in the information age.

What Happens if You Register a Business Name or a Pty Ltd Company? What Rights Do You Get?

In Australia, the business name or Pty Ltd registration does not give you the protection of your proprietary and intellectual property interests. The Business Name legislation and the Australian Securities and Investment Commission are concerned with the establishment of a business name and Pty Ltd register of business names and their particulars. They are not concerned with conferring rights or protection regarding such a name. You should, after selecting a business name or a Pty Ltd company name, conduct a thorough search of the

Trade Marks register to make sure that the business name or Pty Ltd company is not similar to any registered mark.

Business names and Pty Ltd names are best protected from exploitation when they are registered marks. On the other hand, your new business or Pty Ltd name may infringe a registered trademark. Research the trademark database before registering a new business name or a Pty Ltd company name.

What is a Trademark?

A trademark can be a word, phrase, number, letter, sound, smell, shape, logo, picture, an aspect of packaging, or a combination of these. It is used to distinguish the goods and services of one trader from those of another. A registered trademark gives you the exclusive right to use, license, or sell it within Australia for the goods and services for which it is registered. Trademark registration is not compulsory, but it is advisable. There is protection against misrepresentation under the trade practises or fair trade legislation. It is also possible to take action under the common law, but this can be a time-consuming and expensive exercise. Registration of a business, company, or domain name does not give you proprietary rights — only a trademark can give you that protection.

The same word(s) can be registered by different people as business names and trademarks. However, the registered trademark owner can sue the business owner for infringing the trademark if the business name owner uses the trademark on goods or services similar to those covered by the trademark registration.

What About Domain Names?

In current times, besides deciding on business names and trademarks, a trader also has to consider the registration of a domain name to protect their intellectual property. The rules for registration of a '.au' name used to be strict. Since 1st of July 2002, the ability to register domain names under the '.au' has been relaxed significantly. See http://www.melbourneit.com.au for the latest information on registration of domain names.

AVAILABLE AUSTRALIAN DOMAINS AS OF 2011

.com	Available to any individuals, organisations, or companies.
.net	Available to any individuals, organisations, or companies.
.org	Available to any individuals, organisations, or companies.
.info	Available to any individuals, organisations, or companies.
.biz	Available to any individuals, organisations, or companies.
.com.au .id.au	For individuals.
.asn.au .info.au	Available to everyone for information exchange.
org.au	Available to a registered non commercial organisation.

Consult an IT specialist and your lawyer regarding protecting your internet intellectual properties. There are many cases where a trader forgets to register their domain name to protect their business names. There are cyber squatters in cyberspace. These cyber squatters check to see if your business name is registered as your domain name. If not, they quickly register the domain name and then offer the domain name to your business later at a price.

There are many things to consider when going into business. Always get legal advice to ensure you do not make an expensive mistake. Be daring, but be careful!

Entering Into a Business Partnership

Sometimes, you may find that although you wish to become self-employed, you may not have the funds to set up your own business. You might have considered having a partner to share the expense, the load, and the risk. That may often be a good idea, as two heads are better than one.

However, there are several things to consider, as having a partner can be like entering a marriage. These are the essential questions you must answer before you make your decision.

Do I need a partner?

There are many good reasons to take on a partner. If the partners contribute equal capital, then pooling resources makes sense. However, that is not the only good reason for a partnership. These scenarios can also be profitable:

- One person intends to invest all the capital while the other will be contributing his skill.

This has the potential to be profitable for everyone, provided both parties sit down with a lawyer early on to place a financial value on the person's skill set.

- You and your potential partner have complementary skills. For instance, one is a financial expert and the other an ace at managing employees. This could be an excellent way to begin a new venture.

- You are opening a business with family or friends. This can be a mixed bag. On the plus side, families are experienced at working side by side and may have a shared long-term vision. On the other hand, running a family business is hard work and lots of responsibility. To decide whether your friends and family will be a blessing or a curse, you need to think of the company as a legal entity first. Running the company is about legal obligations and responsibilities, not fun. If you and your prospective partners can't see beyond the familial bonds, it may be best to keep business out of your relationships.

What is the partner going to do for the business?

Before you get married, you should sit down with your spouse and decide how your relationship and lives will work. Likewise, the first thing you should do when planning a legal partnership is to decide all the details. How much money will each person contribute? What responsibilities will each person have? How many hours will each person work? Who will handle the money? How will profits be divided? What if one person wants to take a bigger draw of income? How will the daily operations be divided?

An experienced attorney can help you sort through these issues right from the start. I ask my clients to go through checklists that will define roles and expectations. Besides helping you create the legal entity, this process starts a necessary dialogue between partners about the direction of the company. And, just like in a marriage, the best time to talk is when everyone is optimistic and eager to start rather than waiting until disputes arise.

Should I have a partnership agreement?

Yes! As the American Express advertisement says, "Don't leave home without it!" Do not start a partnership without a written partnership agreement. If you take the details for granted, you will have trouble. I once advised two brothers and their wives who wanted to open a restaurant together. I asked them basic questions, such as who would be running the kitchen, who would be working with employees and serving customers, and who would be handling the finances. The parties refused to even talk about how they would divide the labour. "We are family, we will work it out," they insisted. Unfortunately, three months later, one brother came to see me. The business was in serious trouble because of conflicts between the four partners. The brothers were no longer talking to each other. It ruined the entire family.

Why didn't the family heed my advice to begin with? Well, people don't always see the value in hiring a lawyer until something goes wrong. And most new companies are low on resources and not eager to spend $2,000-$3,000 on legal services right away. However, it is much cheaper to treat the sickness before it occurs than to wait until there are major conflicts, and you wind up in court. Lawsuits are very expensive. In Western Australia, if a dispute is not covered by a partnership agreement, unfortunately, it falls under the Partnership Act. The overwhelming majority of these cases must, therefore, be heard in the Supreme Court. The cost of taking a case to the Supreme Court is at least $20,000, and that is before you even have your day in court!

What if I want to dissolve the partnership?

The partnership agreement should agree what the partners will do if one or more partners leave and the company dissolves. Dissolution could occur because of retirement, an argument, or death. I was involved in a case where one partner died, and his wife wanted to take his place in the partnership. The other party objected. There was no partnership agreement to address the situation. The result was a very messy court case.

Arguing about how to dissolve a partnership is doubly damaging to the value of the company because there is no one around to run the company while you and your partners slug it out. Besides paying legal fees, the business is crippled if not destroyed.

The partnership agreement can be structured almost any way you want it. If death occurs, like the one mentioned earlier, the contract could give the surviving partner a certain amount of time to buy out the surviving spouse. Problem solved. If one partner retires, the agreement may stipulate that his stake in the company goes up for auction. Again, problem solved. The partnership agreement puts you in control of your destiny, not the courts. If you remember one thing about partnerships, it should be *an ounce of prevention is worth a pound of cure.*

Tips for Buying a Business

If you *do* have enough money to start your own business, you might buy a business from someone else rather than starting from scratch. I have these ten points for you to consider if you ever strike out on your own.

1. Sign no offers to buy any business until you have received legal advice. The lawyer should help to draft the conditions of purchase that will protect you.
2. Make sure there is a clause to allow your accountant to check the figures. This ensures that the business income is as represented by the seller. Many sellers do not tell you the full story about their finances.
3. Make sure that any employees that continue to work with you have had all their long service and other leave benefits paid out.
4. Have a clause that allows you to check the business turnover before you purchase the business.

5. If the business is a franchise, make sure that the contract is subject to your lawyer approving the franchise terms.

6. List all assets that come with the business. If the printer or signage is supposed to be included, make sure it is listed in the schedule.

7. Ensure that you have a clause to allow you to opt-out if the lease terms are not favourable. There is no point in buying a business if the lease for the premises will expire soon.

8. If you are financing the purchase, update the vendors regarding the finance approval.

9. Discuss what business structure you will use with your accountant. This should be done before you even make any offers. See my advice on business structures.

10. Ensure you are happy with your settlement date. Will everything be ready by then?

Many other minor details can make your purchase a breeze. As always, when in doubt, speak to a lawyer.

Get Yourself a Raise! Ray's Ten Rules of Negotiation

If you do not want to be your own boss, do not be embarrassed. There are many good reasons to be an employee, including benefits, time off, and more balanced home life. Realising that your work goals do not include self-employment is a good thing. It means you have thought through many of the questions I raised earlier and decided to remain an employee.

The top complaint most people have about their current job is their salary. Most people feel they are not paid enough. However, according to a recent survey by Accenture, less than 50% of people ever ask for a raise! I know you may be saying, "Ray, there is a global recession that is not only depressing wages, it is causing many people to lose their jobs." I do not want you to be out of a job. But there are opportunities for growth, even in a recession.

So what is the art of negotiation? I suppose the main lesson is that "if you do not ask, you will never receive." The Accenture survey also revealed that 85% of people who ask for a raise received something of value! The numbers broke down this way:

- 38% said they got the raise they wanted.
- 25% said they got *more money* than they expected to get.
- 17% said they got more money, but not quite as much as they wanted.

- 5% did not get more money, but they did get some other incentive that made their job better.

I'm sure you will agree that an 85% chance of improving your situation means it is worth asking for a raise. You may still fear being fired just for asking the question. But when you think about that fear without emotion, you will realise that the odds of this happening are slim provided you go about it the right way.

Negotiating is like playing poker. You do not know what the other side is ready to accept. It is obviously easiest if you are unemotional. They say emotion is an irrational master. Remembering that, here are my ten rules for negotiating that can be applied to any situation that arises in your life:

1. *Be unemotional.* If you are emotional, get someone else to negotiate for you. In your job, it helps to run your argument by your immediate supervisor and enlist their help in going to the main boss.
2. *Always know your bottom line beforehand.* And always ask for more than your bottom line in your first offer.
3. *Try to discover as much as possible what weaknesses the other party has.* Are they under

pressure to retain and promote people with master's degrees? Do they lack employees with the same skills as you? Has prior turnover hurt the company? When you know what they are worried about, you can sell yourself as the answer to their problems. If you are negotiating the sale of a property, try to figure out whether they need to sell. Are they time poor? In any situation, the other party has a weakness you can exploit.

4. *Do your research first regarding the value of anything you are negotiating on.* Often, when a company has laid off a lot of workers, it increases the value of the existing workforce because the remaining employees are now doing more than just one job. If you are the person asked to pick up the slack for the ten people the company fired, then you will probably find it is much cheaper for the company to pay you to do the work of ten people, even with a raise. Using research, you can show the company how much money you save them, and saving money is valuable no matter what the economic climate.

5. *Do not be afraid to walk away from the deal.* This is normally thought about in buying and selling deals but consider this scenario. Imagine your boss threatens to fire you for

asking for a modest raise, and he or she refuses to even consider giving you perks that cost the company nothing. If that happens, then you have learned something important about the company you work for. You have discovered that they are not the right company for you. You will have the impetus to polish off your resume and look for a job with a better future. Resist the impulse to be a doormat!

6. *Know the main actor.* There is no point in negotiating with someone who is not making the decisions. You may think that the supervisor of your department is the person who decides which employees get a raise, but the reality could be that the department head only acts on recommendations from below or above. Lawyers experience this all the time during mediation processes. For example, the defendant may be the person who we are seeking a settlement from. However, sometimes I discover that the insurance company decides whether to settle and for what amount. Do reconnaissance to discover who is in charge.

7. *Be creative with the way the deal will work.* Think of all the permutations that can work for all parties. Write down all the

permutations before negotiating. There are many ways to structure raises. Think of some perks that will cost your company virtually nothing, like different start time, extra holidays, upgraded equipment, etc.

8. *Avoid negotiating where there is stress on time or anger issues.* You need a calm, controlled environment to negotiate. Writing things down ahead of time will also help you control your nerves.

9. *Ask questions of the other party as by asking questions you get to know what the other party wants.* If you can give it to them, the deal can be closed. When negotiating a raise, discover what the employer believes makes a great employee. Once you get them to lay out what matters to them most, you can explain why you meet those standards. Likewise, if you are negotiating over the sale or purchase of property, don't be afraid to ask questions and frame your offer to meet their needs.

10. *The most important part: Never be embarrassed to make the final 'ask'.* Let's say the other party just told you their 'final offer.' If you ask one more time if they will settle on your final position, the worst that can happen is that the other party says no. But if you do not ask, you will not know. You lose nothing by

making one final counteroffer. You might be surprised by how much more you get.

Negotiating is something that we have to do all our lives. We negotiate with our spouses, our kids, our bosses or workers.

Everything is negotiable.

The more we learn the art of negotiation, the better we become. Good luck!

CHAPTER 4

A Great Estate - What You Owe Your Family

A t one time, there were three generations living under my roof. There was my wife, Annie, and my two sons, along with my mum and Annie's mum. The boys have kept me occupied with their many sporting activities, mainly golf, badminton, tennis, cycling, and swimming. A father brings up his child knowing, one day, that his child will, hopefully, exceed the father in all the father has done, including sport. I have now reached major milestones with both my sons beating me at different sports. Jazton defeated me at badminton at the age of 11. He continues to go from strength to strength, including representing the Bronze medal winning Western Australian Under 19s State team when he was just 15 years of age. He has represented Western Australia in several state teams. He plays golf and is at a ten handicap, much to the annoyance of his jealous dad. My favourite days at the golf course are when he is playing by my side. I am sure many fathers enjoy a golf game much more when they are walking down the fairway with their child, discussing their life and future.

My son, Tyzton, beat his old man at swimming at the tender age of nine. I recall I had finished a long day at the office when Tyzton asked me to take him to the pool. He was always persistent, which is one trait I loved about him (although it was always a test as to who could wear whom down).

Tyzton told me he would swim ten laps with me. Ten laps? I was surprised because in all the times he went to the pool with me, he just wanted to fool around. I had seen him swim a lap at most, but it was always after great persuasion. I humored Tyzton and brought him to the pool.

I told Tyzton we would do a lap of freestyle. If after one lap he did not want to swim anymore, I would be disappointed. After two laps, to my surprise and delight, he was still swimming and finishing laps right behind me. After the next lap, he caught up with me. I had never seen him swim that well before.

Try as I might, I could not beat him on the next seven laps. He won fair and square.

The feeling of pride in my younger son was a real awakening. That moment, I realised my child had grown and learned all I had taught him and was now doing better than his teacher and father.

Our children have been raised with the presence and guidance of our extended family. My sons both earned their tae kwon do black belts by the age of ten. This achievement can be attributed to the patience of my mother-in-law. She drove them to all their classes and sat through hours and hours of training before my sons graduated. To honour her, my family is commissioning a picture frame with all my sons' coloured tae kwon do belts.

My late mother-in-law was such a great grandma to my children, picking them up every day from school and making a quick meal for them when they were hungry. My wife and I would not have managed the legal practice as efficiently as we did if we did not have my mother-in-law's help every day. She passed away in 2012 after suffering from dementia. She lived with us until she was taken to the hospital and passed away peacefully. Because of her short-term memory loss, she believed every day was the eve of the Chinese New Year. The celebration of the coming

New Year emphasises washing away the bad fortune of the past year and welcoming the new one with wishes of peace and happiness. What a blessing to be stuck in that time warp.

Are there challenges to living with a loved one losing their mental faculties? Of course! But we would not have had it any other way. It was my honour to care for the woman who gave me my wife and cared for our family so selflessly. Which brings me to the point of this chapter: What do we owe our families?

My sons, Jazton and Tyzton, with my wife Annie and her mum.

Estate Planning

With family values, the cultural differences between East and West are perhaps at their most glaring. East Asian countries have been profoundly influenced by Confucianism, which prioritises taking good care of one's aged parents as the most important societal and moral value. This duty is reflected and reinforced in Chinese law.

Most East Asia Pacific countries today still see aged care as the responsibility of the extended family. In the mid-1990s, Singapore enacted the *Maintenance of Parents Act*, enforcing that traditional value. Singapore holds children legally responsible for supporting their elderly parents. Parents can even sue their children for not providing care. In countries like Malaysia, the government subsidises services such as daycare to enable adult children to financially support their ageing parents.

Nations influenced by English common law have a different conception of filial responsibility. Australians agree that they should help their elderly parents. However, they are not as willing to accept measures such as living nearby or with their parents, limiting their working hours, or other actions that constrain their personal freedom. And elderly parents generally agree with this approach. Is it in

Western culture that many older Australians do not believe that it is the duty of younger family members to provide help to elderly family members? Many believe that a person has an obligation not to be a burden on their adult children.

Under Australian law, if you do not take charge of your own estate planning while you are alive, you risk having the government and their appointed trustees — who don't know you or your wishes — do it for you. To leave your family in the best position possible, you owe it to them to set up an estate plan long before you become elderly.

So what is estate planning?

- .It is planning for the future management and distribution of your assets. It is also planning for your future medical care and lifestyle choices if you can no longer decide due to illness or accident.
- It is a way of ensuring that your estate is passed onto your beneficiaries in the most financially efficient and tax-effective way possible.
- Most people do not think about what would happen to them if they became incapable of deciding due to an accident or illness.

- If you don't have an estate plan, the person who may be appointed to deal with your financial affairs, make lifestyle choices for you, and be the guardian of your minor children may not be the one you would have chosen.

- The potential number of people who can bring a claim against your estate is getting larger thanks to legislation changes introduced in 2013. Your stepchildren are included in the new classes of persons entitled to challenge your will.

The most important components of an estate plan are Wills, Enduring Power of Attorney, Enduring Power of Guardianship, Advanced Health Care Directives, and Superannuation. Additional things should be considered, so I recommend speaking with a lawyer to get the full story. Or simply send me an email through Tan & Tan Lawyers' free email advice service at ask@tanandtanlawyers.com.

Wills

Once, a husband and wife came to see me to make a Will. They were from Asia and had one son and one daughter. They wanted to leave all their properties to their son. They were from a very traditional, old-fashioned family. I tried my best to explain that what they were proposing sounded most unfair. Here, traditional Asian values had to bend to modern recognition that sons and daughters are equal. I took great pains to explain to them it was not just about only leaving their properties to their son. I told them they had to consider how it would affect the relationship between the son and daughter after their death.

I have seen families break up because of wills that favour different children. I have acted for a 70-year-old mother who had to sue her son because her husband did not make a Will and finalise his affairs before his death.

Lots of problems can be caused by a failure to plan. In Western Australia, the law has a set formula for distributing estates where there is no Will. That formula may not be how you wish your estate to be distributed.

Failure to plan is equal to planning to fail. So, what needs to be considered if you want to make a Will?

The first point is to decide who is to be your trustee/executor. The term is used interchangeably. The job of the trustee is to obtain a document from the Supreme Court. That document is the Grant of

Probate. The Grant of Probate allows the trustee to sell the properties belonging to the estate. The trustee then distributes the estate according to the instructions in the Will.

Whom you appoint as the trustee is a very important matter. The trustee has to be someone you trust as they control your assets. They may well sell everything and disappear to the Bahamas. So choose a trustee you know will not disappear with your estate.

If you have young children, it is also important to choose a guardian who will look after your children until they are adults.

After you have decided who is to manage your estate, you have to decide how you wish to distribute it.

- Do you wish to give everything equally to your children?
- When do you wish them to receive their money?
- What can the trustee spend your money on while your children are still infants?
- What happens if your children and spouse do not survive you? Who gets your millions?

A Will is rarely permanent. Any time there is a major life event, you should change your will. If you get married or discover that you will become a parent, change your Will immediately. In fact, a marriage annuls your Will.

For single parents, a Will is one of the most important things they can have, particularly if the children are young. A Will deals not just with assets, but also with custody of minor children.

You need to make it very clear who the proposed guardian should be if you pass away. If you appoint a friend, make sure they get along with the members of your family. The guardian should also know your wishes for things like schooling and religious upbringing. If you do not think of this ahead of time, interested family members may go to court to challenge the decision.

Most people do not realise that when you remarry, any prior will is cancelled. If one party passes away, the new spouse will normally believe that any assets that belonged to the deceased spouse now belong to the new spouse.

According to the Administration Act 1903, if there is no will, a surviving spouse with children will get the first $50,000 of the estate followed by 1/3 of the estate. The other 2/3 is divided among the children. You may ask why the first $50,000? Well, that was roughly the value of a house in the ancient days in Western Australia when the Administration Act was last amended in 1982. There is a proposed change in the Administration Act 1903 to change the figure to $435,000 instead of the $50,000. However, as at the writing of this book, the laws have not been changed.

Recently, I took on a case where a farmer in order to save money, prepared his own Will. He had quite a lot of money to leave his family. However, the Will was not executed properly, and there was a question as to whether he was actually sane when he prepared it. He had six children, and they all disagreed about who should be appointed executor or trustee. They could not even agree on which one should be appointed let alone how to divide up assets.

Like the farmer, people often believe they can draft their own Will, and it will be valid, even if the Will meets none of the technical requirements of the law. This is not correct. One of the technical requirements is that the Will must be signed by two witnesses at the end of each page. If you had no witness or just one, it is not valid, and the Will can be challenged in court. That is one of many reasons you really should speak with a lawyer before you draft your own Will.

Most lawyers do not charge more than a few hundred dollars to discuss how a Will can be properly done and witnessed.

Enduring Power of Attorney

An Enduring Power of Attorney (EPA) is one example of how the law empowers people to make choices about who may decide matters for them if they become incapacitated.

What is an EPA?

An EPA is a legal document allowing you to appoint another person to make financial and property decisions on your behalf.

A person who makes an appointment under an EPA is called the DONOR. A donor can authorise another person or persons to be their ATTORNEY to act for them if they become mentally ill or lose their decision-making ability.

An EPA differs from a normal Power of Attorney, which only remains valid if the donor can still make decisions. Under an Enduring Power of Attorney, an Attorney can act even after the donor loses their legal capacity.

What does an EPA Authorise my Attorney to do?

An EPA does not authorise your Attorney to do everything on your behalf. It will only authorise them to decide about your FINANCIAL and PROPERTY affairs. An EPA does not cover non-financial decisions—for example, decisions regarding your health care or medical treatment.

If you are unsure about the decisions that an Attorney can make under an EPA, seek legal advice.

Why should I make an EPA?

An EPA is necessary to protect your assets and ensure that they are managed by someone you know and trust if you suffer a mental disability.

If you own any property, consider making an EPA. Losing legal capacity can be gradual or sudden, occurring because of an accident, injury, or through illness or trauma later in life.

It may not be possible to predict or prevent the onset of mental disability, but by appointing an Attorney under an EPA, you will be safeguarding your interests by putting your financial affairs in the hands of someone you trust.

Who should I appoint as my Attorney?

You can appoint anybody to be your Attorney, including your spouse, partner, children, relatives, friends, lawyer or financial adviser. You can also appoint more than one Attorney, for example, where you want your children to act together (or separately) as your Attorneys.

The most important consideration you must make before appointing an Attorney is whether you can trust that person to decide about your financial affairs. Ideally, it should be someone who you know will manage your affairs and decide in your best interests.

I often tell my clients to consider:

If you appoint one of your children to be the attorney, is that child going to put you in the cheapest nursing home or the most expensive? Remember that when you eventually pass away, that child may stand to inherit a more valuable asset if he or she placed you in an 'El Cheapo' nursing home.

What happens if I don't make an EPA?

In Western Australia, if you lose your ability to make decisions and have not appointed an Attorney under an EPA, the State Administrative Tribunal may appoint an Administrator on your behalf to manage your affairs.

Take note that a state-appointed Administrator may not necessarily be someone who you trust to manage your financial matters. You very should consider the need for an EPA to be in place to prevent this possibility from arising.

Usually, an EPA will be preferable because it gives you the power to appoint someone to be your Attorney. The time and cost involved in making an EPA is a small price to pay for your peace of mind.

How do I make an EPA?

For an EPA to be valid in Western Australia, it must comply with the requirements set out in the *Guardianship and Administration Act of 1990.*

In addition, a person making an EPA must be of sound mind when the EPA is made. If there is any doubt as to the mental state of the donor, a medical opinion should be sought to confirm their legal capacity.

Standard EPA forms are available for download on the State Government's website. As a donor, you can complete an EPA yourself, or you can arrange for a lawyer or Trustee Company to prepare the documents for you.

You can also specify in your EPA exactly how you want your Attorneys to carry out their responsibilities. All Attorneys will have obligations under the *Guardianship and Administration Act,* and it is up to you to provide special conditions that apply whenever they decide for you.

If you are unsure about the legal effect of an EPA or what rights and obligations an Attorney has, seek legal advice.

When does my Attorney's appointment come into effect?

An Attorney appointment can come into effect either immediately after the EPA has been signed, or only once the donor has been declared legally incapable of deciding. In your EPA, you must specify whether you want the Attorney to assume power immediately, or whether the appointment will only be valid after the State Administrative Tribunal makes an official declaration you do not have the legal capacity to make your own decisions.

If you appoint an Attorney to act immediately, your Attorney must act under your directions while you are still legally capable. I usually advise my clients to state that the EPA only becomes valid when there is a declaration from the State Administrative Tribunal about their incapacity.

An EPA can be revoked at any time provided that you are still of sound mind when you revoke it.

As we get older, we may need to consider arrangements that can protect our assets if we cannot do so ourselves. As the population gets older, it is imperative that EPAs be considered as early as possible before it is too late.

Enduring Power of Guardianship and Advanced Health Care Directive

In Western Australia, an Enduring Power of Guardianship ("EPG") is a legal document that authorises a person of your choice to make important personal, lifestyle, and treatment decisions on your behalf should you ever become incapable of making such decisions yourself. This person is known as an enduring guardian. An enduring guardian can be authorised to decide about matters such as where you live, the support services you have access to, and the treatment you receive. An enduring guardian cannot be authorised to make property or financial decisions on your behalf.

What kind of decisions can an enduring guardian make?

- Where you live, who you live with, and who you associate with
- Whether or not you work
- Makes treatment decisions on your behalf
- Decides what education and training you receive
- Commences, defends, conducts, or settles any legal proceedings on your behalf, except proceedings that relate to your property or estate
- Advocates for, and decides about, the support services you access
- Seeks and receives information on your behalf.

Like the Enduring Power of Attorney, you need to decide who is the best person to decide for you. If in doubt, speak to a lawyer.

Advanced Health Care Directives

An advance health care directive is a written statement made directly to medical personnel about the treatment you want or do not want to receive if you ever become incapacitated and incapable of communicating your wishes. The treatments include medical, surgical, palliative and dental care. It also includes life-sustaining measures. These are decisions that may be crucial, and you need to decide who is to make those decisions.

An advance health care directive is ineffective after death, Therefore, you cannot record your wishes about organ donation in such a document.

What is elder abuse?

Lately, I have been acting for more clients in elder abuse cases. This is when the children are unwilling to wait for their inheritance. Instead, they abuse their parents in different ways to get their hands on their parent's money before the death of their parent.

Elder abuse is becoming a growing problem as we face an ageing population. According to a report in 2018 by a Select Committee into Elder Abuse (the 'Committee') appointed by the WA State Government, there are around 75,000 older people at risk of elder abuse. Experts believe this is just the tip of the iceberg with many cases going unreported.

The abuse our poor seniors are suffering from are:

a. abuse of enduring power of attorney given to relatives.
b. emotional abuse by preventing parents from having contact with other children.
c. slapping or even burning parents.
d. over medicating or under medicating with a hope that the parent's life will be shortened, so the children get their hands on their inheritance faster.

The list goes on. It saddens me when I have to face these cases. However, I feel more strongly about issues of parental abuse more than anything else in my practise of law. Being a traditional Asian brought up to respect and honour my parents, such cases touch a raw nerve with me.

Elder abuse could happen by placing your father in an all English-speaking nursing home instead of one where the staff speak the language that your father understands and where there are residents of the same cultural background.

I am in a case where an Enduring Power of Attorney and Guardianship was given to a son. The son is now trying to sell the family home and stopping his father from seeing his other children. The other siblings are applying to court to stop the proposed sale of the family home.

Recently I received a call from an old client of mine.

He had previously appointed his second wife as his attorney and guardian in his EPA and EPG. His will also gave the majority of his assets to his second wife.

He informed me that he had been placed in a nursing home by his second wife. He did not want to stay in the nursing and his second wife had removed his credit card and his phone. As I knew his second wife, I gave her a call to try and find out what was happening. She informed me that my client had been diagnosed with dementia by a Dr. X. I then went to speak to my client again to see if he remembered being tested by Dr. X. My client told me he was never tested by Dr. X despite Dr. X providing a detailed report about a test done on my client. Was my client experiencing an episode of dementia?

A quick Google search showed that Dr. X had been suspended by the medical board for charging patients for dementia tests when he never did the tests.

I am now in the process of challenging any suggestion that my client has dementia. If he succeeds in proving he is capable of giving his lawyers instructions, he can change the appointment of his second wife as his enduring attorney and guardian. Of course, he also wants to change his will again due to what his second wife had done to him.

Was this elder abuse?

Hence, you should see a lawyer to discuss your rights, especially whether an Enduring Power of Attorney or Guardianship should be given to any child.

If you believe any seniors you know are being abused, report the matter to www.advocare.org.au

Parents should think hard about whom they are giving their Enduring Power of Attorney or Enduring Power of Guardianship to. Seek legal advice to protect yourself.

CHAPTER 5

Family Relations

I have the good fortune to be married to my best friend and soulmate, my wife Annie. We have been married for nearly 23 years now. She runs the settlement division of my business, manages my practice, takes care of our household, and puts up with my golf and crazy antics. She is my equal and my confidant.

Our life has been one big adventure, especially raising our sons. I gave up golf when our sons were small, so I could devote my energies to spending time as a father. It is very important to find activities that the whole family can participate in. One of our favourite activities as a family is badminton. The boys have been playing badminton with my wife and me since they were about six years old. Our two boys have represented Western Australia in different national badminton championships. Tyzton has also represented Australia as a Junior player.

Badminton is also one thing we used to share with our friends when the children were young. I used to spend my weekends with the same group of friends for many years. We used to play badminton in the day and then play gin rummy at night. All the children have now grown up. However, the bonds created during those early days kept friends and families together.

One reason many spouses split up is that they do not spend quality time together as a family and with good friends. It is difficult getting a group of friends together where the husbands and wives don't share the same mutual hobbies. If the spouses share the same hobbies, a safe bet is that the children will enjoy their hobbies too.

When a couple doesn't have good friends with mutual interests whom they can rely on, there is too much stress on the marriage.

Unfortunately, in Australia, a high percentage of marriages end up in divorce.

Checklist for Couples Contemplating Divorce

For some, divorce may be in their best interest so they can move on with their respective lives. Divorce is still a major decision, which is why I suggest going through the following checklist if you are going through a separation:

1. *Speak to each other to confirm there is no future in the marriage.* You only see a lawyer if there is no other option. You lose nothing by seeing a counsellor. You discover there may be a path to healing the marriage. But if the parties agree that the relationship is hopeless, then a counsellor can give you the tools to end the marriage.

2. *Discuss with your spouse what is to happen with your children.* Agree that, despite the relationship ending, the most important concern is the welfare of the children of the marriage. Too much time and money are spent fighting in courts over children because of anger. Those fights do not help the children.

3. *List assets and liabilities so that when you see your lawyer, you have all the required information.* Obtain documents to show your assets and liabilities.

4. *Prepare a Will.* Instruct your lawyer to immediately prepare a Will, so if anything happens to either spouse during the time the family matters are being sorted out, the wishes of the deceased spouse have been declared.

5. *Consider your superannuation fund.* Inform your superannuation trustee of your updated wishes regarding your superannuation fund.

Property Settlements: Questions and Answers

If you are married to someone and you separate or divorce, you will want to split the property accumulated during the marriage at some stage. This process is called 'property settlement'. Property settlement is the most contested issue in a separation simply because everyone – clients and lawyers, and even judicial officers – have a differing opinion on what is "just and equitable". Have you not encountered a situation where your partner and you cannot agree on what is right or wrong or what is fair regardless of what is right or wrong?

The first question is, what is included in the legal definition of 'property'?

In the Family Court, "property" includes many types of assets, e.g.:

- home or land
- parties' bank accounts
- vehicles
- household furniture
- shares and debentures
- paintings, antiques, and other works of art
- clothing and jewellery
- superannuation entitlements
- businesses
- insurance policies.

Anything that can be given a monetary value is included.

In Australia, you need not be divorced before considering property settlement. You can apply to a Court before your divorce or after. However, you have 12 months after the 'decree absolute' of your divorce to finally file for property settlement. The Court may tell you that you are out of time if you file after 12 months. You can ask the Court for permission to apply out of time if you have good reasons.

Good reasons include that both husband and wife still own joint properties.

If you are in a de facto relationship, then you have 2 years from separation to file a claim for property settlement.

Which law applies?

In Australia, the *Family Law Act (Commonwealth)* and the *Family Court Act (WA)* cover all areas of property division. In Western Australia, if you have been in a de facto relationship, you can now access the Family Law courts.

Should I consult a lawyer?

It depends on the assets you own, but usually, it is well worth employing a lawyer to make sure you get what you are entitled to. Property settlement issues can be very tricky. The effect of a bad settlement may be difficult to change through the Court system.

Getting ready to commence proceedings: what to think about

Sit down and list all the assets you both own. These should include properties solely or jointly owned

Try to include the date and the cost of the purchase of each asset.

Gather as much paper evidence as possible.

Protecting Your Home

The first thing your solicitor should advise you to do if you have a home or any other land is to get an injunction to prevent it from being sold without your knowledge.

If you are joint owners on the title of a home, no one can buy the property without your permission. If the property is only in your husband/wife's name, or the name of a company in which they have an interest, you need to get an injunction from the Family Court to ensure the property is not sold without your consent. A cheaper option is to put a caveat on the title to protect your interest. However, there are rules and limitations as to whether a caveat can be lodged instead of getting an injunction from the Family Courts.

A commission set up by the Law Reform Commission of Western Australia on 2nd August 2016 recommended that a new category of "spouse caveat" be created and that the Family Court of

Western Australia be given express power to extend the operation of the spousal caveat.

At the date of my book, it is still not legislated.

A caveat prevents the Titles Office from allowing the property to be dealt with unless you are notified and given the opportunity to object to any sale or transfer of the title.

It may also be important to inform your bank to disallow any further borrowing on the property.

How will the court decide what is a "just and equitable" property settlement?

The Court will usually place all your properties into one basket and total out the values. Ensure proper valuations are obtained for all your assets so proper negotiations can be conducted with your spouse.

Debts like hire purchase or mortgages will be deducted from the value of the assets. For instance, if a boat is worth twenty thousand dollars, but there are eight thousand dollars left to pay on hire purchase, it will be valued at twelve thousand dollars.

An overdraft, loan, lease agreement, tax debts, credit card balance, and any other outstanding debt will be considered as a liability.

The Court will, therefore, deduct all liabilities from the asset value to reach a lump sum for distribution between the parties.

The next question is how does the Court decide what proportions should be given to each spouse.

Some things the Court may consider:

Pre Marriage assets: The relevance of pre-relationship assets depends on how long you were in the relationship before the separation. If the relationship was short, the ownership of these assets would usually be retained by the person who brought them into the relationship.

The longer the relationship, the more chance that both partners have contributed to the accumulation of the assets. For example, one of you may have looked after the children and the house while the other worked.

Homemaker/Parental contributions if you did not work: The Court recognises contributions made by the person who has looked after the children and home which would have allowed the other person to study, earn a living, or run a business. That one person paid for or acquired the asset is not the only consideration when deciding a party's contribution to the relationship. The Court knows you cannot put a dollar value on the homemaker and parental contributions, unlike financial contributions.

Gifts before and during the marriage: The Court will try to work out the intention of the person who made the gift. For instance, the Court may deem that financial support (usually in a lump-sum monetary gift) provided by a party's parents is to benefit the couple equally, despite the money being gifted to one partner only. That partner may seek to have that gift classified as an indirect financial contribution from that party.

Current and Future Needs: The Court considers the current and future needs of both parties

The Court will have regard to the factors under section 75(2) of the Family Law Act. Without listing all those factors down, bear in mind that the court considers all matters past, present, and future to decide whether an order is "just and equitable".

For example, if the wife is going to be looking after young children from the marriage after separation that may impede her employability or the number of hours worked, this is something the Court will consider.

Do I have to go to Court to get property settlement?

No, but if you want your agreement to be binding, it must be approved by the Court. The Court then makes 'Consent Orders'. These can then be enforced through the Court.

IMPORTANT NOTE:

In Australia, if you are transferring a house to your spouse as part of an agreement, transferring the house will attract stamp duty as if you were buying a house. However, if you obtain a Family Court order, the transfer will attract a minimal amount of stamp duty. That means it may be worth formalising your property settlement by way of a Family Court order to save cost on stamp duty.

How do we do this?

Think seriously about using a lawyer for property settlements. They can help negotiate an agreement and look after all the formal Court requirements.

There are two possible methods to finalise property settlement.

Form 11 Consent agreement

If the parties can agree on how they want to split their assets, a Form 11 agreement can be prepared. The form is rather simple to complete. However, it would probably be prudent to seek legal advice on the drafting of the proposed orders you want the Court to make to finalise your property settlement.

Your intentions need to be properly formalised and worded so there is no confusion as to how your properties are to be dealt with.

The document should usually be signed before a solicitor after general advice on the fairness of the document is discussed.

The Form 11 agreement is then signed by both parties and lodged in Court. The Court will consider whether the agreement is "just and equitable" before making the orders and will not just "rubber stamp" any orders. The orders, when made, are as good as if the parties had gone to a full Court hearing to sort out their property settlement.

What if we cannot agree?

If the parties cannot agree on how to split up their property, then the Family Law rules list out certain procedural requirements that must be complied with before an application can be filed in the Family Law Courts.

These pre-action procedures are in place to help you save money eventually. But often, parties cannot appreciate this as they are emotionally and mentally affected by the separation process.

Before you file an application in the Family Court: Pre-action procedures for financial cases

Simply put, the pre-action procedures comprise of 3 broad steps:

1. Family Dispute Resolution;
2. Setting out your position;
3. Disclose documents.

Family Dispute Resolution

There are 4 main mechanisms for dispute resolution: mediation, negotiation, conciliation and arbitration. The more commonly used are mediation and negotiation. Negotiation usually always occurs at the start when lawyers are involved. All too often, parties unwisely wait till the matter goes to court before attempting mediation, conciliation or arbitration. By such time, the legal costs incurred would be significant. Pennywise, pound foolish perhaps?

Setting out your position

In a perfectly ideal situation, all relevant information is clear and available, and the parties have attended a family dispute resolution in a bona fide attempt to resolve the dispute. However, if they fail to settle, each party can identify their positions regarding the other and put it down in writing. Not uncommonly though, in a less than perfect world that we live in, each party will exaggerate their entitlements and positions at this stage hoping to concede at some later stage. Any 'genuine offers' to settle aren't usually all that genuine, at least from a client's subjective point of view.

Disclosure of documents

You have to exchange your documents relevant to the dispute prior so the parties can ascertain the accuracy of their claims and of the other party. If you fail to provide adequate disclosure, not only will this delay proceedings, you also risk the wrath of the court. The court considers it important that each party is "totally honest and open about their financial situation".

The duty of disclosure starts at the pre-action procedures and ends when the case is finalised. You cannot choose when the duty of disclosure should apply to you or the other party. Neither is the duty of disclosure conditional upon the other party complying with the duty. Some clients think that is unfair, especially when they have complied with their duty. Of course, people who provide scant disclosure or avoid giving full disclosure, do so to obtain some sort of tactical advantage. This may be so at the pre-action procedures. Unsurprisingly, the end result is one party commencing a claim in the Family Court.

What happens when the application is filed in the family courts?

To commence a claim, an applicant must lodge in court a Form 1 – Initiating Application, Form 13 – Financial Statement and a supporting affidavit, then serve these documents to the other party.

To respond to a claim, the respondent must do likewise.

The first court return date is allocated within 2 months of the initiating application. At that hearing, where you and your lawyer have to be present, you inform the court what steps the parties have taken and also identify what further actions are required, such as further disclosing documents or undertaking valuations of the parties' assets.

If the court considers that the parties have a modest asset pool, you will likely be allocated a date for a conciliation conference. The conciliation conference is where all parties meet with their solicitors (if any) and a Registrar who acts like a mediator. The Registrar's job is to get the parties to settle their matter out of Court.

Because the court has limited resources, conciliation conferences are allocated to those parties' whose asset pool are relatively limited or small. For those with a larger asset pool, the court expects that the parties will have the resources for private mediation.

In my experience, about 70% of cases settle at the conciliation conference stage. The other 30% may progress to a full trial before a judge. Even though a matter is set for trial, the parties can still negotiate an out of court settlement at any stage. I would say that of the 30% of cases that proceed to be set down for trial, another 20% of overall cases settle just outside the Court doors before the trial proceeds.

The balance of the 10%, where the parties cannot agree, is decided by a Judge, after a full hearing of the life history of the parties. Unfortunately, by the time the matter reaches a Judge, both parties would have spent considerable funds and experienced a lot of anguish.

Depending on the asset pool, sometimes it is wiser to settle earlier than later. Money aside, so often litigants forget there are other "unseen" costs, such as time, effort, emotional and psychological decay, that should have been factored in from the start. Pennywise, pound foolish again?

Court approved property settlement

After a Form 1 is filed, the Court can consider an out of court settlement. The Court will look closely at your agreement and assess whether it meets the legal principles relevant to property division. Just because you are happy with the agreement, does not mean the Court will be.

Matters the Court will consider:

- whether the agreement is fair to both of you; and
- your specific circumstances, such as your age, health, income, assets, and liabilities, etc.

It's difficult to change a property agreement once it's approved. Courts try to make sure that they get it right the first time. By using a lawyer, you have a better chance of the Court accepting your agreement because the lawyer will understand the Court and the Court know that you have obtained independent legal advice.

We often say that the only person who wins because of feuding parties, especially in a matrimonial matter, are the lawyers. Therefore, find a lawyer who is looking after your interest and not looking to prolong the matter. Feel comfortable with your lawyer, and trust he or she is doing everything to help resolve your problem as effectively as possible.

To cut a long story short...

We once acted for a European lady involved in protracted negotiations with her Asian husband on property settlement matters. There were obviously cultural differences, which resulted in their estrangement. To say the negotiations were unfriendly would be an understatement. There was a lot of anguish and acrimony between the two parties. Luckily, both the other lawyer and I knew that it would cost both parties a lot of money to get the matter to a final hearing simply because of the anger they had for each other.

We got the matter to a pre-trial conference. To make sure the parties did not get at each other's throat, the other lawyer and I kept them on two floors at the Courthouse. The other lawyer and I walked up and down the two levels, going between the two estranged spouses from 9 am to 5 pm while the negotiations were in progress. It was one settlement where the parties argued over who would take the salt and pepper shaker.

Fortunately, the matter was settled out of Court without the parties having to go to trial. They may have spent 8 hours (with a lunch break) negotiating on every item of their property, but it was still less expensive than if the matter had gone to trial.

I suppose the matter would be very different if both lawyers were impatient and pushed the parties to go to a trial to resolve their differences.

Moral of the story: Make sure your lawyer is looking after your interests as best as he or she can and not let anger and emotion cloud your better judgment.

Even if your lawyer has done the best for you, there is no guarantee that an upset partner will not try to do something outside the law.

I recall a case regarding property settlement where my client insisted that the court order state that a tablecloth handwoven by his sister be returned to him.

The ex-partner agreed, and the court order stated that it was to be handed over to my client. The problem was his ex-partner returned it to him after cutting the tablecloth into two pieces. What can he do? Bring the wife back to court for contempt of court? It was just not worth it. However, it shows what an angry ex-partner is capable of.

De Facto Relationships

According to surveys and the census taken recently, the number of persons in de facto relationships is steadily increasing.

Although most of the other States have recognised de facto relationship rights for years, Western Australian law gave very limited rights to parties in de facto relationships. Issues regarding children could be argued in the Family Court. However, if a de facto relationship breaks down or one partner passes away, there was no formal process for resolving disputes over property and maintenance.

The only avenue for any de facto couples if they wished to argue about property rights was to go the

Supreme Court. Everyone knows that to go to the Supreme Court means big bucks.

Fortunately for Western Australians, 1st December 2002 saw a radical change in the law. Persons in de facto relationships can now apply to the Family Court for resolution of their family problems.

It is better to apply to the Family Court as it is much less expensive and is confidential. It also provides access to alternative dispute resolution processes.

These laws only apply to de facto couples whose relationship ended after 1st December 2002.

Because of the current laws, if you can show you have been in a de facto relationship for at least two years, you can:

- Apply to the Family Court for property and maintenance orders.
- Contributions made towards the accumulation of assets will be considered compared to the previous law where, for example, if your name was not on a property, you could not claim an interest in the property.
- Parties can be ordered to go for mediation and counselling.

To fall within the current laws, the first point is to show you have been in a de facto relationship. In making that assessment, the courts will consider these matters:

- Whether the parties have been together for over two years.
- Whether the parties lived in the same residence.
- The degree of financial dependence, or the financial arrangements, between the parties.
- The ownership, use, and purchase of the parties' property.
- Whether there is, or has been, a sexual relationship between the parties.
- Commitment by the parties to a shared life.
- Whether the parties care for and support children.
- How the parties' relationship is perceived by others.
- The age of the parties. Generally, the parties should be at least 18 years of age.
- Whether one or both of the parties are usually residents in Western Australia. The requirement is that both parties must have lived in Western Australia for at least 1/3 of the period of their relationship.

It does not matter whether:

- The people are of different sexes or of the same sex.
- Either person is legally married to someone else or in another de facto relationship.

If you can prove the existence of a de facto relationship that falls within the Act, the Family Court can make these orders to resolve property disputes and maintenance issues.

Maintenance

One of the most important rights that has been granted to de facto spouses is the right to claim maintenance. If a former partner cannot support himself or herself adequately, for example, if the applicant has the care of a very young child or a young disabled child, then an application may be made for maintenance.

Matters the Family Court will consider include:

- income, property, and financial resources of each partner;
- the physical and mental capacity of each partner for suitable employment;
- financial needs of each partner;

- responsibilities of each partner to support someone else; and
- terms of any property adjustment order.

The court may only make a property and maintenance orders in three situations:

- Where the parties have been in a de facto relationship for at least two years.
- Where there is a child of the partners of the de facto relationship who is less than 18 years of age and serious injustice would result to a partner; or
- Where the applicant substantially contributed to property and serious injustice would otherwise result.

The matters that the Family Court must consider before making any orders to adjust property rights include:

- nature and length of the relationship;
- direct and non-direct contributions made by each partner to the welfare of the other partner or a child of the partners;
- age and health of each partner;
- direct and non-direct contributions made by each partner;

- income, property, and financial resources of each partner; and
- earning capacity and financial needs of each partner.

How about my rights if my partner has passed away?

Another big impact of the current law is the right of a partner whose de facto spouse has passed away. The laws will allow de facto partners to make claims against the estate of their deceased partners.

What do I do if I am in a de facto relationship?

The legislation provides an opportunity for de facto couples to make agreements that will reduce the impact of the defacto family laws. They can do so by signing agreements similar to pre-nuptial agreements.

If a de facto couple has entered into a recognised financial agreement, then the agreement will be enforceable by the court. The problem is how you broach the subject of signing such an agreement without affecting the relationship in a negative way.

In certain circumstances, even though an agreement attempts to nullify the effects of the new laws, the court can still vary such an agreement if:

- there is serious injustice or,
- where there has been a material change in circumstances
- it is impractical for the agreement to be carried out.

If you have questions regarding the current laws, consult a lawyer to see how your property rights have improved or how your property rights have been eroded (depending on which side of the coin you are at).

Modern Marriage or de facto relationships and the Binding Financial Agreement

Let's say you are about to commence a serious relationship with a partner. You have assets, and your partner has nothing. What should you do to protect your hard-earned assets? You may have heard about the prenuptial agreements fashionable in Hollywood. Would a prenuptial agreement work for someone who is not a superstar? It may be hard for you to believe, but the answer may actually be yes. Here are simple guidelines for determining if binding financial agreements between partners are right for your situation.

What is a Binding Financial Agreement?

In 2000, Australia finally permitted the use of binding financial agreements. A binding financial agreement deals with how property and belongings are to be divided if a breakdown or separation occurs in a marriage or defacto relationship. The agreement can be entered in one of three stages: 1) before the marriage or commencement of the defacto relationship as a prenuptial agreement; 2) during the marriage or the defacto relationship and before divorce or separation; or 3) after the marriage or defacto relationship to prepare for divorce or separation. Couples who plan to live together can make a cohabitation agreement to protect their assets even if they have no intention of getting married.

I am about to enter a marriage with a partner who hasn't got many assets, but I have an investment property. What can I do to protect myself?

This is the classic case to have a binding financial agreement prepared before the marriage. It is always more difficult to sign a binding financial agreement after the marriage. A lawyer should be able to advise you on the best way to secure signing a binding financial agreement, so a subsequent separation will not impact on your investment property. There are other situations where a binding financial agreement is an obvious solution, such as:

- When cohabiting, couples move into a house owned only in one person's name. The person who owns the property may wish to make sure that their partner will not benefit from the property on separation.

- Another situation would be where one partner's parents gifted them a house, and they do not wish the partner to benefit from it if the marriage breaks down.

- Where one couple is entering a second relationship, they can use a binding financial agreement to protect the assets they gained from the first relationship and also make sure that any children from the first relationship are adequately provided for.

This is obviously not an exhaustive list of situations, but just a few where the use of a binding financial agreement would be a benefit.

What are other benefits of a binding financial agreement?

The main advantage can be described as changing a forced, rushed decision into a well-planned and a considered solution. There is high certainty as you and your (ex)partner can contract out of the Family Law provisions, and you both get to decide on what is fair without letting a stranger do that for you. An agreement will also stop ill-feeling from motivating one person in the relationship to take the other person's assets as revenge. It can reduce stress in a stressful and upsetting time for the two partners.

How do you make sure binding financial agreements succeed?

The first step is to see a lawyer, as you and your partner must get independent legal advice before the agreement is signed. Your lawyer will advise you whether the agreement is to your advantage or disadvantage and whether it is prudent to sign. A contract will then be drawn up and signed by you and your partner, at which time, it will become binding. Your lawyer can explain the technicalities of the agreement to you.

Will this agreement cost a lot of money?

Yes, but less than what it takes to go to a trial. The cost will depend on the individual circumstances of your case, so you would be best served by talking to a lawyer about what the probable cost would be. Although these agreements do involve up-front costs, they will save you money eventually. The fees to finalise a binding financial agreement will cost between $2,000 and $5,000. Consider, however, if there is no binding financial agreement, you can expect to pay thousands of dollars in legal fees.

Can anything change or end the agreement once it has been made?

The short answer to this is yes, but the circumstances have to be exceptional. The court can set aside the agreement if the formalities I described earlier are not complied with. The court also has the power to set aside the agreement if it was obtained by fraud (for example, if your partner hid millions of dollars in a Swiss bank account).

Likewise, if there has been a change in circumstances, and it no longer makes sense to enforce the agreement, the court has the power to make the agreement void. It can also be set aside if there has been unconscionable conduct from you or your partner (if, for instance, one partner forced the other to sign the agreement on their wedding day). The agreement can also be changed if enforcing it would create a hardship on you or your partner.

What if you simply change your minds? Are you stuck with the agreement?

No, this is not the case. You and your partner can enter into a termination agreement if you don't want the binding financial agreement to be used. Both parties must sign the termination agreement, and the binding financial agreement will not be in effect.

If you and your partner have children, will it affect the agreement?

Yes, this would be a significant change in circumstance that will lead the court to void the binding financial agreement. The primary caregiver of the child would be given monthly maintenance that reflects the cost of bringing up the child. The agreement could be changed by you because of the birth of a baby, so the maintenance that is due is certain.

Will the agreement only affect you if there is divorce or separation?

No! The agreement will be considered if you or your partner dies during the relationship. The agreement will be in force between the living partner and the deceased's representative. This means that any special provisions made for the children will still be upheld, and the assets of one partner will not automatically be given to the surviving spouse.

What other assets can be covered by a binding financial agreement?

Many assets can be included in a binding financial agreement. Let's say you are inheriting a sum of money. The agreement can say you do not wish the inheritance to be part of the separation settlement if you and your partner break up. The agreement can also deal with superannuation and can split the superannuation fund between two partners if it is fair to do so. It can also deal with spousal maintenance, so if one partner has less earning capacity because of the marriage, the person can be given money either in a lump sum or periodically to make sure there is no financial hardship.

Should I get a binding financial agreement before or during my relationship?

Yes. That would be a very sensible thing for the parties to do especially when the parties are at a stage, presumably, where they can make important decisions in a mature manner, and where there is, presumably, a high level of trust between them. Further, in creating certainty at separation, which I say is often lacking, the parties have a foundation to plan and move on from. Unsurprisingly, parties encounter difficulties trying to negotiate this topic while they are entering into or in a relationship as the thought of having a binding financial agreement usually evoke a sense of distrust. I strongly recommend parties to overcome that unease. Think about it this way: would the parties be in a better position to negotiate a financial settlement if they separated on unhappy terms? I wouldn't bet on it.

Family law cases are the most difficult to manage in terms of expectations and final results. There are so many variables so that any advice we can give to a client regarding a final outcome may sometimes be limited.

You should understand your rights and the steps you can take to protect yourself before and after marriage or before you commence that defacto relationship.

Hopefully, this chapter will have given you an insight as to what to consider to protect yourself.

CHAPTER 6

Immigration

A ustralian identity has always been driven by immigration and migration. Australia was a sparsely populated continent of less than 750,000 Aboriginal people when the British Empire began colonisation in the eighteenth century. At almost any point in its history afterward, roughly 25 percent of the total population has been born somewhere else.

In the nineteenth century, Europeans and Chinese joined the migration Down Under. But in the early twentieth century, people from countries fighting against the British in World War I were declared 'enemy aliens', while those from Asian nations were completely banned from migration.

World War II brought another change in immigration patterns. After the war, the immigration restrictions relaxed, eventually eliminating discrimination based on country of origin. In the last fifty years, the immigration policy has evolved from the official 'White Australia' policy to multiculturalism, keeping with Australia's location in the Pacific Rim.

Not everyone is happy with multiculturalism, however, and the government sometimes panders to these sentiments. Change is difficult, particularly when it means welcoming different races and people with different religions to the table. Though everyone is the same regardless of origin, my experiences participating in the CEO Sleep-out on behalf of Saint Vincent de Paul show how important it is to walk in somebody else's shoes. The CEO Sleep-out is a charity event that raises funds to help the homeless people in Australia.

My old Wellington Street office has an external toilet. One day, I found a homeless person sleeping there. He would come in after dark and leave the toilet in the morning when the staff arrived. He must have been sleeping there for over 2 weeks until I had no choice but to remove him.

It was emotionally difficult removing the homeless person. It saddens me that there are now homeless people in Perth, which is supposed to be one of the richest states in Australia. Coming from a family of ten, by the sheer determination from my parents, the children are where they are at now. Hence, I have a soft spot for the homeless, as my family could easily have been in that position if not for government housing in Singapore.

For the last 10 years, I have participated in the sleep-out to help those in need while experiencing the physical and mental rigors the homeless endure. With the generosity of my friends and clients, I have been able to raise nearly $300,000 for Saint Vincent de Paul in their fight to help the homeless. I will probably sleep out at the annual event for the foreseeable future, and it is an event that should continue to gain momentum if everyone chips in.

The 14th Dalai Lama teaches that all people want the same things: to be happy and loved, and we are all connected to each other. The differences we perceive between the homeless and ourselves, like those between native-born Australians and newcomers, are not real. I hope as people continue to interact with new immigrants, they will realise this essential teaching is true.

There are so many categories of visas that can be applied for in Australia. I will mention two categories we often deal with at Tan and Tan Lawyers.

Spouse Migration Tips

Now that we've traversed the sad landscape of family dissolution and divorce, let's switch gears to something that should be more uplifting: spouse migration. You have found love finally or again! What to do next?

Spouse migration is fraught with uncertainty, as you suddenly defend the legitimacy of your relationship to total strangers who work for the government! That is the price you pay for falling in love across the border.

I often deal with spouse migration in my work as a registered migration agent, and I have acted for clients who deal with the Department of Home Affairs (DHA) in Australia when they try to bring loved ones into the country. These clients are applying for a spouse visa on behalf of their partners.

From my experience, the DHA's basic concerns when deciding spouse migration applications are:

- that the marriage or defacto relationship is not genuine;
- Somebody is paying a local resident in Australia to enable them to enter the country;
- that an Australian citizen is being duped into marrying somebody who does not intend to remain in the relationship for the long term.

In their daily work, the DHA comes across many cases where they encounter the above issues, so unfortunately, the starting point for the DHA is one of mistrust.

You may have a loved one you have been communicating with on the Internet, or perhaps there is a special person whom you met on holiday and stayed in touch with. These long-distance relationships are very difficult to maintain; I have been through that frustration. However, if you have decided you want to move the relationship to the next stage, then here are helpful tips on what comes next.

First, you have to make sure that when you apply to the DHA, the right information is given. The most important information that the DHA requires is confirmation that the relationship is genuine.

Keep on file information to verify your relationship, such as records of all telephone conversations, letters, postcards, or birthday cards sent to each other, copies of all email messages and anything else you can imagine.

The DHA is also interested in your financial position as a couple, so bank statements showing the joining and merging of expenses are great evidence, along with confirmation you have rented or lived together, such as lease agreements or even letters sent to spouses from government offices.

Photos of you as a couple in many environments can strengthen your application and support your statements.

Above all, appoint a migration agent to assist you in your application. A migration agent is experienced in preparing or submitting what the DHA requires to make a proper decision. The migration agent you employ should organise a mock interview before you are interviewed by officers of the DHA, as this is where a lot of applicants can make mistakes. A simple and innocent issue regarding when you first met can become a major issue in the eyes of the interviewing the DHA officer.

So, what has this article got to do with romance? Well, I pride myself in putting down in words the feelings of my clients when they file their application for a spouse visa. Many clients are not experienced in putting down their thoughts or their feelings in writing, or perhaps they are unsure of how to word their statements to achieve the best outcome.

When the DHA sees an application devoid of any emotion, they are less likely to believe that the love you feel for your partner is true. A good migration agent should ensure that the story you are telling the department is accurate and believable.

When your application is filed, one requirement is a statutory declaration from both parties outlining how the relationship developed, and where the relationship is going. After reading a statutory declaration prepared by myself on behalf of a client, his comments were, "I did not know I loved my wife so much until I read what you wrote."

Based on my experiences, I have been able to describe the romantic element of any application to the DHA. If that romantic aspect is missing from any application, it may cause the DHA believing that the relationship is not genuine.

Hence, if you hope to go forward with the relationship you have been nurturing on the Internet, or marry that dreamboat you met on your holiday overseas, see a migration agent to assist you in being united in Australia with your loved one soon.

I had a farmer client who applied to bring his newly married wife over from his country of birth. He put in the spouse visa application himself and did not do it properly. The application was rejected, and he came to see me to help appeal the decision to the former Migration Review Tribunal. The problem is that the usual time for processing a spouse application is about 12 months. If the application fails, the appeal takes another 12 months. Usually, during these periods, the spouse may not come into Australia if the application is lodged from overseas.

At the appeal hearing, the client cried in front of the Tribunal Member, who was a lady. The Tribunal Member was so moved by my client's tears, she granted my client's spouse the visa. And so, my client's spouse entered Australia, and I thought that was a happy ending.

Except, a few months later, my client came to see me and told me he wanted to kill his spouse. While the application and appeal process were taking place and the spouse was stuck in her home country, she had developed a relationship with another man as a Plan B, just in case her eventual appeal was lost. Now that her spouse visa application had succeeded, she decided that she wanted to bring her Plan B partner into Australia. I told my client he should NOT contemplate committing any criminal act no matter how upset he was. This was advice I was giving him as his migration agent and as his lawyer.

Immigration Using the Business Skills visa

Australia's Business Skills Program is always changing. The focus is on encouraging successful business people to settle in Australia. These migrants are expected to use their proven business attributes to develop business activity in Australia.

Australia has an increasingly global economy, and the government knows that to compete, they need to attract good business migrants.

Many of these migrants bring into Australia their knowledge of business networks, their cultural practices, business experience and, contacts.

Often, they speak languages other than English and enhance the cosmopolitan feel of Australia.

Business migrants benefit Australia by:

- developing international markets
- transferring capital and making investments
- creating or maintaining employment
- exporting Australian goods and services
- introducing new or improved technology
- substituting Australian-made products for goods otherwise imported
- adding to commercial activity and competitiveness within sectors of the Australian economy.

What is the Business Skills Program?

I do not intend to go through the different investment skills visas that are available now as they keep changing. There are many Business skills visas.

Usually, you start with a temporary visa that may be granted if you pass certain points tests. The best place to get all the information is at https://www.businessmigration.wa.gov.au/business-migration

Depending on what assets you have and your business background, a lawyer or migration agent should be able to identify the best business skills visa you can apply for. It also depends on what your business plans are in Australia.

Age is always an issue as many of the visa conditions require that the applicant be younger than 55 years of age. If you qualify, you get a temporary visa allowing you to live and do business in Australia.

Let's take, for example, a subclass 188 visa called the Business Innovation and Investment (Provisional) Visa. The conditions are:

a. You are nominated by an Australian State government.
b. For 2 out of 4 years, you have owned a business with a turnover of AU$500,000 in each 2 years.
c. You must have a significant ownership interest in the business you nominate.
d. You must have personal and business assets valued at AU$800,000.
e. You score 65 points on the points test.
f. You are under 55.
g. You must have functional English and meet health and character requirements.

A lawyer or migration agent should be able to verify all the above requirements for you to ensure that you qualify. The biggest issue is getting documentation to prove these requirements.

We often have potential applicants saying they qualify and, on paper, it seems they do. However, on closer examination, the applicant may not produce concrete evidence to prove they own the shares in the company they have nominated.

It is crucial to see an experienced migration agent or lawyer to ensure the application is flawless. If there are flaws and the application is rejected, the appeal process can take a long time and impact your life substantially.

Conversion to permanent visas

Many of the business skills temporary visas give you an option to convert to a permanent visa. It depends on how much you have invested in Australia. There are too many variables and too many criteria to be discussed in this book.

For example, if you obtained a Visa class 188, you can apply for a permanent visa Class 888 after:

   a. owning up to 2 businesses in Australia for at least 2 years.

b.   For 2 years before applying for the permanent visa, you have held a substantial ownership interest in the business or businesses.

c.   The business you nominate has a turnover of AU$300,000.

d.   For 12 months before you apply, you and your partner have assets valued at AU$600,000.

e.   The business has two full-time employees.

f.   You meet the health, character and language skills requirements.

These are but two of the available business skills visas. See a lawyer or migration agent with your business resume, and see which category they can fit you in for a valid application.

Is migration law challenging?

No area of the law is boring. In my years of practise, I have seen all aspects of human nature. Recently, I was recounting to one of my junior lawyers one of my most memorable experience as a lawyer.

I was asked to represent three clients arrested and detained by the Immigration Department, as their visa had expired, and they were illegally in Australia. I will not mention which country they came from. *The Migration Act* allows a detainee in the detention centre to apply to be released on the agreement that the detainee will arrange to leave the country. To allow the detainee to be released, the Immigration department usually requires a surety to sign a bond to say that if the detainee fails to leave as agreed, the bond will be forfeited. The bond amount can be up to $20,000.

The three clients I saw at the detention centre informed me they had been on the run for over two years. I also discovered that the 'snakeheads' (the people smugglers) would arrange for their clients to arrive in Australia on a valid visa. Upon the expiration of the valid visa, the client would disappear underground. For the privilege of the snakeheads making the arrangements, the clients would pay up to a year's wage to them. Upon paying up the debt to the snakeheads, any time spent in Australia earning an income was a bonus. That bonus could mean the funds to buy a house in their homeland.

For us privileged residents in Australia, it makes you appreciate what we have here.

Two of the three clients were brothers. They all applied to be released on the understanding they would arrange to leave Australia. Their applications were rejected as the Immigration Department did not believe they would abide by their promise to leave Australia. However, the decision is appealable to the Migration Review Tribunal (now an appeal is to the Administrative Appeals Tribunal).

This was where I came in. I was instructed to file the appeal on behalf of the three clients. Upon receipt of my fees (yes for such cases, you need to make sure your fees are paid up-front), I filed the requisite appeals.

The Migration Review Tribunal then set a date for the hearing of the appeals for the three clients. I attended the Tribunal hearing that day for the clients.

Before the hearing, the clients had all arranged for sureties willing to put in a cash bond to confirm they would breach no conditions for their release to freedom (albeit just to allow them to arrange to leave the country).

The hearing was heard by video link as the Tribunal Member for the appeal hearing was based in Melbourne. We attended a courtroom with television screens for us to communicate with the Tribunal Member. As there were three cases, there was a different Tribunal Member for each hearing.

My clients were brought to the court by security guards. The guards were tasked with bringing them from the detention centre to the court and back. There were three guards, one for each client.

The hearing started, and I represented the 1st client. He was not convincing as his record showed that he had been evading the Immigration department for over 2 years before he was caught. The Tribunal Member for his hearing indicated that he did not believe the client would leave the country if he were released. The Tribunal Member reserved his decision, and the client was released from court and taken back to the detention centre by his allocated guard.

I then had to attend the hearing for the next client, who was one of the two brothers. The hearing commenced before a new Tribunal Member. The Tribunal Member, as expected, raised questions as to why he should believe that my client would leave the country voluntarily. I told the Tribunal Member, we had a surety who would place a bond of $10,000 if needed to ensure my client leave Australia voluntarily. The Tribunal Member was not moved and indicated so. Upon realising that the Tribunal Member was not likely to grant my client his temporary freedom, he stood up and said, "I guarantee I will leave the country with my life". This was stated in his native language. Before there was a chance to translate to the Tribunal Member, this client took a razor (God, knows where he got it from and how he sneaked it past security) and slashed his wrist in front of everyone.

There was blood everywhere. There was blood on the table, on my files, on the floor of the court. There was pandemonium as the Tribunal Member screamed out in surprise, and the guards rushed to my client. An ambulance was called, and the security guards tried to stop the client from further bleeding, but he refused to be helped. It took at least 30 minutes before the ambulance arrived and removed the client. However, during all this commotion, his brother made an escape by leaving the building. So it was all pre-meditated. Let's sacrifice one brother to return to their homeland. The other brother can still make money before he is caught again.

That is the extent that people will sacrifice to be in Australia. Being a migration lawyer is not boring. You would be surprised what someone will do to live in Australia.

I had always wanted to be a doctor. I always (for egoistic reasons) wanted to be where a patient would say "Thanks, doctor, you've saved my life". However, that was not to be as I faint at the sight of blood. Hence, I thought the next best thing was to be a lawyer. That is where I am today. I am still happy to know I have helped a client, whether to save their business, their life if it is a criminal matter or their children.

CHAPTER 7

Blunders,
Mistakes and Accidents

"I didn't know what I was thinking!" How often have you slapped your palm to your head and said that to yourself in agony after you've made a boneheaded mistake? Sometimes, we act without thinking, usually because we mean well or want to do something. This chapter will discuss some (but by no means all) of the trap doors we are liable to fall into.

Now, I'm not telling you that by reading this chapter you will avoid all blunders, mistakes and accidents as that's impossible. However, this might prevent you from running headlong into some of the most common mistakes that can cost you dearly.

Do You Really, Really Want to be a Guarantor?

Imagine someone in your life wants you to act as a guarantor for a loan. Whether it's for tuition, a car, a home, or even a line of credit, you need only to sign a contract, typically drawn up by a bank. Should you do it?

I agree that it seems like the simplest thing in the world. Your son asks you to act as a guarantor to the bank to purchase a property. Your son is fairly responsible. He pays his bills, and despite one or two incidents that caused him to have bad credit, you want to help him. You do. He's your son. So what's wrong with that?

Well, let me give you an example. The banks usually require a solicitor to provide independent legal advice before they will allow a loan to be drawn. I once looked over the proposed loan documents and discovered that the son had failed to inform his father that as part of the guarantee, the bank also wanted the father to include the father's property as security. Maybe the son did not even know that his father's property was in jeopardy. Such are the problems when one doesn't read the paperwork. Upon being informed as to the contents of the guarantee, the father declined to stand as guarantor.

Moral of the story: know what you are signing. The fine print needs to be carefully considered. What does it mean to be a guarantor? A guarantee is a contract whereby one person agrees with another to pay some debt or perform some act or duty owed by a third person. This third-person remains, however, primarily liable for such payment or performance and the person giving the guarantee will only become liable on the default of the third party.

The parties to a guarantee contract are:

- The Creditor: The person receiving the benefit of the guarantee is called the creditor. This is usually the bank, finance company, supplier or lender.
- The Principal Debtor: The person borrowing the money or obtaining the benefit of the contract.
- The Surety or Guarantor: The person who provides the guarantee is called the surety or the guarantor.

For a contract of guarantee to be enforceable, it must be in writing and signed by all the parties. For example, if you are providing a loan to a friend 'A', it is not enough for 'B' (the person to guarantee the loan) to say he will guarantee the loan. It must be in writing.

The extent and nature of the liabilities of a surety or guarantor will depend on the words of the contract of guarantee. Some guarantees are limited for a fixed amount. Some guarantees are for an unlimited amount. Whatever is alleged as guaranteed, the court will interpret the contract of guarantee strictly, and a surety will not be liable beyond the precise terms of his or her commitment.

An example: A surety's guarantee to find a replacement tenant for a shop at a specified rental for a term of three years was satisfied by the surety finding a person willing to become a tenant on the prescribed terms. The surety is not held to guarantee the solvency of the replacement tenant or the conduct or performance of the replacement tenant.

Sometimes, there may be two or more persons who enter into a contract of guarantee. The liabilities of the sureties or guarantors are usually joint and several. This means that when there is a default by the principal debtor, the creditor may take action either against one or both of the sureties.

An example: B, C & D guarantee to pay Z a sum of $100,000 if X cannot pay Z. X defaults. Z sues B only because B has assets, sufficient to meet the debt.

B cannot say it is unfair and demand that Z sue all the guarantors as they should be jointly liable.

However, after B has paid $100,000 to Z, B may claim contributions from C & D in whatever proportions they have agreed upon.

What are your liabilities as a guarantor?

After the guaranteed debt has become due, but before the surety or guarantor has been asked to pay for it, the surety or guarantor may require the creditor to call upon the principal debtor to pay off the debt.

After the debt is due, the surety or guarantor may apply to the creditor and pay him off. Upon being provided with proper indemnity for costs, he may sue the principal debtor in the creditor's name, or in his own name if he has obtained an assignment of the guaranteed debt.

As soon as the surety or guarantor has paid to the creditor what is due to the creditor under the contract of guarantee, he is entitled to 'step into the shoes' of the creditor and avail himself to all the rights possessed by the creditor in respect of the debt, default or miscarriages to which the guarantee relates.

Thus, upon payment, the surety or guarantor should have the benefit of all the securities that the creditor has received from the principal debtor.

For example: Where the guaranteed debt is secured by a mortgage executed by the principal debtor, the surety or guarantor is, on payment of the debt in full, entitled to transfer the mortgage to themselves.

The surety or guarantor also has rights, either express or implied, against the principal debtor or his estate for indemnification. The rights include the ability to recoup the amount that the surety or guarantor has actually paid for the principal debtor with interest.

Discharge of the Guarantee

Payment made by the principal debtor of the guaranteed debt will normally discharge the surety or guarantor.

Common instances of the need to provide a guarantee

(a) An incorporated proprietary limited company seeking a business overdraft facility or loan. The Bank providing the overdraft facility or loan will call upon the directors of the company to stand as sureties or guarantors.

(b) An incorporated proprietary limited company leasing office premises. The landlord will require the directors to stand as guarantors for the performance of the lease.

(c) When a family member wishes to buy a property and has insufficient income. A person with an alternative source of income and with assets may be requested to stand as a guarantor.

Often, you may receive a request to stand as a guarantor. The first thing to ask yourself is whether you really should do it. The answer depends on assessing the risk involved and the person you will guarantee. If in doubt, the best course is to decline to be a guarantor. If you cannot decline, then the next best thing is to limit the guarantee. Whatever it is, seek legal advice. Understand the legal consequences of acting as a guarantor. Before signing on the dotted line, it is advisable to consult a lawyer so he can explain to you your rights and liabilities.

Think Before You Drink and Drive

One Saturday night two years ago, my wife and I were having dinner with another couple, and the four of us shared a bottle of red wine. We did not even finish the bottle, though I must admit, I had more than the other three drinkers. I drove home instead of getting the missus to drive as it was a short trip, and I was sure I was under the limit.

Suddenly, while driving back home from Victoria Park to Kensington, I saw the flashing and blinding lights of a police wagon. I pulled to the side and got out of the car.

Yes, it is always better to get out of the car so you can have a friendly chat with the cops to see what you have done. I find that sitting in your car while being questioned usually causes more tension.

It is usually intimidating dealing with the law even though I am a lawyer and well versed in criminal law. This is especially true when you are the suspect.

The two officers said they did not think I was turning the car properly when I turned right into Berwick Street. The next thing I knew, I was being breathalysed.

The reading was just above 0.05, which is an offence liable to a fine and demerit points, but no suspension for a first offence in Western Australia.

I was then asked to return to the Kensington Police Station, where I was to be tested again on one of their more sophisticated machines. I was worried when I stepped into the police paddy van as I knew I may have committed an offence. It is a drink driving offence and should be taken seriously as many accidents have happened because of drunk driving.

Once you are sitting inside a police paddy van, life takes on a different perspective. There are no cushions or seat belts, and there is only a small window you can look out of. I am sure there was also no air conditioning. My mind immediately flashed back to a case where an Aboriginal elder collapsed in a prison van while being transferred to Kalgoorlie in stifling heat. He died a short time later in hospital.

Luckily for me, the ride was just two minutes. At the station, I had to wait for over half an hour before the machine could take my reading. I had a good chat with the police about the law and their side of it compared to my perspective of it.

My final breathalyser reading was finally done, and the reading was 0.059. However, the police then reduce the reading by the time of your last drink, under the Western Australian, ROAD TRAFFIC ACT 1974 - SECT 71, which states:

ROAD TRAFFIC ACT 1974 - SECT 71

71. Blood alcohol content at material time, how it's calculated

1. In any proceeding such as is mentioned in section 70(1) a person's blood alcohol content at any time which is or may be material in the proceeding (the *material time*) shall be calculated having regard to —

    a. the time of the person's last drink containing alcohol taken at or before the material time; and

    b. the material time; and

    c. the time at which the sample of the person's breath or blood was provided or taken for analysis (the *time of sampling*); and

    d. the person's blood alcohol content at the time of sampling,

    so as to give effect to the presumption that after a person's latest drink containing alcohol the person's blood alcohol content increases at the rate of 0.016 g of alcohol per 100 ml of blood per hour for a period of 2 hours and, after that period, decreases at the rate of

0.016 g of alcohol per 100 ml of blood per hour.

2. For the purpose of making a calculation under subsection (1) in any case where any one or more of the times referred to in that subsection can only be ascertained as falling within a period of time, the calculation shall be made taking such time within that period as produces the result most favourable to the person charged.

3. For the purpose of making a calculation under subsection (1) but subject to subsection (2), in any case where the time of a person's last drink containing alcohol is not ascertained, the time of the person's last drink containing alcohol shall be taken to have been such time as produces the result most favourable to the person charged.

4. In any proceeding such as is mentioned in section 70(1), the concentration of alcohol calculated to have been present in the blood of a person at any time under the preceding provisions of this section shall be conclusively presumed to have been present in the blood of that person at that time.

Based on the assumption I had my last drink one hour ago, the reading was reduced by 0.016, which brought my reading of 0.059 to below 0.05 – or 0.43 to be exact. This is called the count back rules. This meant I had not broken the law by drink driving.

With a handshake to my police friends, I bade them goodnight as my wife Annie was waiting for me to drive home. I was glad to have been able to experience part of the process of drink driving arrests. I was even more relieved that I did not have to go through the whole process of being charged.

Please note that this count back rule has since been removed on 11 September 2019.

I do suggest to my friends and clients that drink driving offences are very serious offences as they can cause the loss of lives or injury. They can also result in financial hardship, especially when you cannot drive to work.

In Western Australia, any person who commits a 0.08 drink driving offence automatically gets a 3 month suspension. For certain categories of drivers, including holders of an Extraordinary licence or novice drivers, the tolerance is zero. The court system does, however, allow a person disqualified to apply for an extraordinary licence. These licences are getting harder and harder to get as the courts get serious about drink driving.

However, the best lesson is that if you drink, you should not drive.

What to Do After a Motor Vehicle Accident? Whether You are the Injured Person or the One at Fault

For many years, Tan and Tan Lawyers have represented clients involved in accident matters. We have represented clients in the criminal courts because of the client being prosecuted for traffic offences. We have also represented clients in personal injury claims.

The saddest cases are when young drivers or passengers are injured because of some silly mistake. Mistakes that could affect a young life forever. We once acted for a 17-year-old foreign student who became a tetraplegic after a very serious accident. The case was settled out of court, and our client received well over $1.5 million dollars. However, no amount of money could compensate him for the inability to walk again.

With that in mind, here are matters to know after an accident.

This information is important if you were the driver of a motor vehicle and the collision injured anyone or damage to property. If you have been involved in a traffic accident, seek legal advice quickly.

Your Responsibility as a Driver

You must stop immediately if you are the driver of a vehicle involved in an accident, and anyone is injured or property is damaged. ('Property' includes your own and other motor vehicles, houses, fences, gardens, personal belongings etc.)

You must give your name and address to anyone who has been injured or whose property has been damaged.

What to Do at the Scene of the Collision

Take these steps:

- Note the names, addresses and insurance details of any other drivers involved in the collision;
- Note the details of the other vehicle involved;
- Note the names and addresses of any witnesses at the scene;
- Draw a sketch of the scene and note the street names and suburb;

- Do not under any circumstance admit that the accident was your fault.

You Must Report the Accident to the Police

If the police do not attend the scene of the accident, the driver MUST report the accident to the nearest Police Station immediately if anyone was injured or the estimated value of damage to property was $1000 or more.

When police officers attend the scene of an accident, or when you report the accident to a Police Station, provide:

- Your name, address and drivers licence details; and
- The name and address of the owner of the vehicle.

If your vehicle is involved in an accident (whether or not you were the driver), you must give to the Police Officer any information you may have that may help to identify the driver.

What You Do Not Have to Do

You DO NOT have to supply any other information, make a statement, fill in any forms, or provide a sketch plan of the scene if you do not wish to.

You legally report the accident. You are not under any obligation to provide any information regarding how the accident happened.

The mistake made by many drivers is in providing full details to the police about how badly or wrongly they had been driving their car. You are only giving the police information to prosecute you with.

If You Receive a Summons:

You may receive a summons from:

1. The Police alleging that you have broken the traffic laws OR
2. a summons or a writ claiming the cost of repairs from the owner of the other vehicle.

If you receive a summons, obtain legal advice immediately.

Repairs to Your Vehicle

The cost of repairs to your vehicle may either be claimed from the owner of the other vehicle, claimed on your insurance policy, or paid for out of your pocket.

Claim against the other party:

If you believe that the accident was caused by the driver of the other vehicle, you should obtain at least two written quotes for the cost of repairs and send them to the other party or to their insurance company with a letter requesting that the cost of the repairs be paid for.

If this request is refused, you may have to sue the other driver. Obtain legal advice before you do so.

Claim against your Insurance Company:

Inform your Insurance Company about the accident as soon as possible. Whether you can make a claim will depend on the insurance policy you have.

Payment from your own pocket:

If you accept that the accident was your fault and your vehicle is not insured, you must pay for the repairs yourself. The other driver may also claim against you for the cost of repairs to his/her vehicle. Consult a lawyer before considering making a payment. The law considers contributory negligence. That means the other driver may partly be in the wrong. Therefore, you may not have to pay the full cost of the damage.

What to Do if You are Injured

In Western Australia, if you have been injured as a pedestrian, passenger or the driver of a vehicle, you may claim compensation for your injuries from the Insurance Commission of Western Australia (ICWA).

Give the ICWA notice of your claim as soon as practical after the accident. You do this by completing the ICWA claim form. If you see a solicitor, they will inform the ICWA for you and provide ICWA with all necessary information in your favour. ICWA will then investigate the accident and statements will be taken from drivers and witnesses.

What Can You Claim?

The money paid to a person injured or has suffered loss is called DAMAGES.

There are two categories of damages:

Special damages, which includes items such as loss of wages, medical and surgical fees, hospital fees, and various out of pocket expenses. It may also include loss arising from damage to clothing or other property.

General damages, which is monetary compensation for such things as pain, suffering, loss of earning capacity, and loss of enjoyment of life generally.

Often, a loss of earnings claim can be substantial. For example, you may be a 30-year-old gardener earning $500 per week, and you receive injuries that prevent you from working as a gardener. If you work as a shop assistant, earning a reduced income of say $300.00 per week, your potential loss of income is $200.00 per week until retirement age. The court may compensate you your total loss of income after considering matters like the early payment of your damages claim and the value of such funds being given to you immediately.

What must an injured person prove?

Not everyone who is injured in an accident may have damages. The right to damages depends on some other person being at fault in either causing or contributing to the accident. All the circumstances of the accident will be looked at to decide whether a driver was at fault. An accident may have been caused by some fault of the person injured and the driver. There, the responsibility for the accident will be divided between them. The damages will be reduced.

A passenger is usually faultless of any negligence, and they can make a claim for damages. However, if you are a passenger in a car driven by a drunk and you were aware the driver was drunk, the court may refuse your claim as they may consider that you accepted the risk of sitting as a passenger in a car driven by a drunk.

You must always obtain legal advice about your claim for damages.

Insurance companies work because most victims do not know their legal rights, and therefore, make no claims for compensation after an injury. For those who are astute enough to make a claim, the insurance companies will try and pay as little as possible to finalise the claim.

I once acted in an accident matter where the client had moderate injuries, but there was also a moderate loss of income claim. When my client first wrote to the insurers, they offered her $500 to settle. When we acted for the client, the insurers offered to settle for $3,000.00. By the time a summons was issued against the insurers, the offer jumped to $30,000.00. When the matter went to a pre-trial conference, the matter was finally settled out of court for $90,000.00.

The client would have obtained much more if the matter went to trial, but the client was happy to take the $90,000.00 as it was far higher than any amount, she thought she could claim.

Party on, but not with blinders on!

I have sometimes written articles for magazines. Typically, the editors select a theme, and then I write my article with that theme in mind. Once, a magazine asked for an article centred on the carnival. We all like a good time and letting our hair down— even lawyers. However, as a lawyer, I can't help thinking about the other side of a good party, which happens at a carnival or party when something goes wrong. Whether it is a party at a business or in a private residence, certain matters need to be considered to make sure we do not get sued and have a massive hangover.

Here's a Q and A that should get you thinking next time you are planning that New Year's Eve bash in Western Australia:

Can you sue the host if you are injured at a party?

Answer: Yes. You need to show that the host failed to carry out his or her duty of care and that the host has breached the *Occupier's Liability Act*. The occupier's liability is defined as the liability to compensate injured persons because of the premises' dangerous condition.

The *Occupier's Liability Act 1985 (WA)* provides for the situation of an occupier negligently injuring an entrant in relation to a static condition of the premises or activities conducted on that premises. *Occupier's Liability Act 1985 (WA)* s. 5 provides that the occupier owes a duty of care to persons entering the premises.

So, for example, if you are at a party and the balcony collapses, you have a claim against the host. The host will then pass the claim on to the insurers. Hence, hosts of parties should always make sure their insurances are up to date.

What is your legal responsibility as a host?

Answer: It depends on whether you are a guest or a trespasser. The basic law is that you are responsible for reasonable foreseeability of a real risk of injury to an entrant or to the class of people to which the entrant is a member. The measure of the discharge of duty is what a reasonable person would do under the circumstances in response to the foreseeable risk.

So, if you have guests in your home and there is a gaping hole in the backyard, you must cover the hole to make sure no one falls in and also warn them of the hole. However, the duty will be different if a burglar breaks in and falls into the hole in the backyard, as you have no legal duty or responsibility to the trespasser.

What are your rights as a host of a party regarding property damage by a guest?

Answer: You have a claim against the person who damages the property. But will you sue Uncle Ben for breaking that vase?

Can the host of the party be held responsible for underage drinking, even if the host did not provide the alcohol?

Answer: It is not illegal for a person under 18 to drink alcohol in a private residence. However, as the adult supervising a young person drinking alcohol in a private home, you are legally considered the host, and as such, are responsible for that person. As the responsible adult, you must take care to look after those under your supervision.

Party crashing: What are the host's legal rights?

Answer: Given that the party crasher is uninvited, he becomes a trespasser. The trespasser can be asked to leave, and the police will usually assist. However, the host should immediately ask the party crasher to leave or else the party crasher is deemed to be a guest.

Is the duty of care between a social host and a licensed venue very different?

Answer: Yes, as the law stands, the owner of licensed premises who makes a profit out of serving alcohol has a higher duty of care compared to the host of a party who makes no profit. However, see the case of

C.A.L. No. 14 Pty Ltd v. Motor Accidents Insurance Board; C.A.L. No. 14 Pty Ltd v. Scott [2009] HCA 47, which has cleared up much of the law.

Am I accountable for anyone who becomes unwell due to consuming food/drink at my party even if the food/drink has been professionally catered?

Answer: If the food is professionally catered, the guest makes a claim against the caterers. The law, until recently, was that if the owners of licensed premises allow a guest to drink to a state where they are a danger to themselves, they were liable. However, in 2009, in a decision called C.A.L. No. 14 Pty Ltd v. Motor Accidents Insurance Board; C.A.L. No. 14 Pty Ltd v. Scott [2009] HCA 47, it was ruled by the High Court of Australia that publicans have no general duty of care to protect patrons from the consequences of getting drunk. There was essentially no duty for a publican to protect their drunken customers from themselves.

A duty of care negligence claim was DISMISSED against a Tasmanian hotel owner who handed back motorcycle keys lodged for safekeeping to an insistent, belligerent patron, who upon leaving the pub, was killed in a crash while showing a blood alcohol level of 0.253.

The licensee and the patron had agreed that the patron's motorcycle and keys should be held by the licensee, and the patron's wife called when the patron was ready to leave.

The man had been served seven or eight cans of bourbon and cola between 5:15 and 8:30 p.m. The licensee told him he had had enough, that it was time to go home, and asked for his wife's phone number so she could fetch him. The patron became agitated and said, "If I want you to ring my f'ing wife, I'd f'ing ask ya."

The licensee responded, "Whoa hang on, whoa, whoa, whoa, this is not, ya know, don't go crook at me, this was not the arrangement that was made." Not having the wife's phone number, and not wanting to push the issue into further confrontation, the licensee then gave the keys to the patron, after asking him three times if he was OK to drive. The man did drive and killed himself.

This case has been hailed as a victory for common sense.

The Court found there is no general duty of care, saying:

"Outside exceptional cases, which this case is not, persons in the position of the Proprietor and the

Licensee, while bound by important statutory duties in relation to the service of alcohol and the conduct of the premises in which it is served, owe no general duty of care to customers which requires them to monitor and minimise the service of alcohol or protect customers from the consequences of the alcohol they choose to consume."

The three judges, with whom a fourth agreed, stated:

"Expressions like 'intoxicated' 'inebriation' and 'drunkenness' are difficult both to define and to apply. The fact that legislation compels publicans not to serve customers who are apparently drunk does not make the introduction of a civil duty of care defined by references to those expressions any more workable or attractive."

The judges commented:

"Persons who serve drinks, even if they undertake the difficult process of counting the drinks served, have no means of knowing how much the drinker ingested before arrival. Constant surveillance of drinkers is impractical. Asking how much a drinker has drunk, how much of any particular bottle or round of drinks the purchaser intends to drink personally and how much may be consumed by friends of the purchaser who might be much more or much less intoxicated than the purchaser would be seen as impertinent. Equally, to ask how the drinker feels, and what the drinker's mental and physical capacity is, would tend to destroy peaceful relations, and would collide with the interests of drinkers in their personal privacy."

So, in summary, what is the takeaway from this article? Have your party. However, make sure you have insurance. Although the law, as it stands, is on the side of protecting the hotelier or licensee, the law can always change if the circumstances warrant it. Each case is different, and you cannot prevent a guest from trying their luck at changing the laws by challenging the precedent set by <u>C.A.L. No. 14 Pty Ltd v. Motor Accidents Insurance Board; C.A.L. No. 14 Pty Ltd v. Scott [2009] HCA 47</u>. For those of you who host wild parties in the privacy of your own home or those who are still young and determined enough to test the boundaries of decency, try making those parties a sleepover, eliminating the worry about drinking and driving entirely.

Conclusion

I hope you have enjoyed reading about my experiences in the law. I have seen much human nature in over 29 years of law practise, which has given me anecdotes that can make you laugh or make you concerned about how low human nature can be. I have acted for multi-millionaires, prostitutes, and drunks. I have acted for public listed companies and small businessmen. I have acted for mothers, fathers, and then their children. I always tell them I want to protect their interest and save them money. That is my practice motto.

Life is a constantly evolving matter. Enjoy the company of those next to you. Appreciate what your life has given you. There is an old Chinese proverb, "If a man compares himself to others, he will compare himself to his death". That is because wherever you are, whatever your station in life, someone is always better off than you, and yes, someone is always worse off. So, enjoy your life.

I did ask quite a few friends if the title of the book was racist. Many laughed and said it was not racist as it was written by a Chinese person in a Western world. Yes, I am the yellow person between the Black and White of the legal system.

About the author

A n Asian lawyer practising law in Australia for over 29 years. Raymond has always believed that it is an honour to protect the legal interests of his clients. Many of these clients have become friends. Raymond is based in Perth, Western Australia and, his Tan and Tan Lawyers offices are at 6/78 Terrace Rd, East Perth WA. Raymond became the first Asian Public Notary in Western Australia when he was appointed on 19 December 2003. Raymond's favourite charity is helping the homeless. He has participated in the St Vinnies CEO Sleepout for 10 years. This is an event where Raymond sleeps out for a night as a homeless person to raise funds for the homeless. He is also a keen golfer and badminton player. Raymond is also a keen blogger. His law blog is called The Perth Asian Lawyer.

Author's note

Thank you for reading my book. I hope the book has assisted you in gaining some understanding as to how the legal system works in Australia. If you wish to leave any comments or feedback, please send me an email at ray@tanandtanlawyers.com

Please feel free to leave a review of this book.

Yours in good faith;
Raymond W H Tan.

Thank You !

Thank You For Reading My Book!

I really appreciate all of your feedback, and I love hearing what you have to say.

I need your input to make the next version of this book and my future books even better.

Please leave me a helpful review on Amazon letting me know what you thought of the book.

Thank you so much!
Raymond W. H. Tan